# AMERICA'S
# HIDDEN SUCCESS

### REVISED

*John E. Schwarz*

# AMERICA'S HIDDEN SUCCESS

*A Reassessment of Public Policy
From Kennedy to Reagan*

REVISED

*W. W. NORTON & COMPANY*
*New York    London*

Library of Congress Cataloging-in-Publication Data

Schwarz, John E.
   America's hidden success. Revised.

   Includes index.
   1. United States—Politics and government—1945–
I. Title.
JK271.S355   1987      320.973      87–13743

ISBN 0-393-30447-7

W. W. Norton & Company, Inc., 500 Fifth Avenue, New York, N.Y. 10110
W. W. Norton & Company Ltd., 37 Great Russell Street, London WC1B 3NU

1 2 3 4 5 6 7 8 9 0

*To Judi, and to Jodi, Jennifer, and Laurie, with Love*

# Contents

# List of Graphs and Tables

*In political arithmetic, two and
two do not always make four.*

Alexander Hamilton
*Federalist*, No. 21


*If all others accepted the lie which the Party
imposed—if all records told the same tale—
then the lie passed into history and became
truth. "Who controls the past," ran the Party
slogan, "controls the future: who controls
the present controls the past."*

George Orwell, *1984*

# Preface

In one fashion or another the past has a way of intruding on the present and the future. This is what must happen, for as Alexis de Tocqueville explained in his *Democracy in America,* when "the past has ceased to cast its light upon the present and the future, the mind of man wanders in obscurity." Yet exactly how past experience will influence us necessarily depends on the understanding we have of that experience. Since this is so, our understanding of the past requires close and continuing scrutiny to ascertain whether it correctly reflects the actuality of the past or some mistaken set of stereotypes and myths.

History, of course, is vast, so that virtually all of its topics embrace a great range of possibilities. Such is the case with the topic of this book, which centers on whether our perceptions of the performances of our government and economy over the past three decades accord with the reality. I do not claim to cover the whole field. My focus instead is on a series of widely accepted impressions of the inadequacies of the government and the economy over the past generation or more. Standing for many years at the forefront of conservative thought, these impressions increasingly entered into liberal and independent thinking, too, as the 1970s drew toward a close. While other concerns about the record of our government and economy over the recent past could have been singled out as the focus of examination, and might have suggested different conclusions about the past, the ones I have selected were chosen because they have been uppermost in the minds of the American public and at the vortex of the nation's debate during each of the last two presidencies, those of Jimmy Carter and Ronald Reagan.

My objective is to provide a perspective enabling readers to question whether or not key assumptions commonly made about the nation's performance over the last thirty years truly reflect reality. I do so hoping that this perspective will help us make greater sense out of what now seems to be a puzzling and terribly disappointing era of our history, and equally important, that it will enable us to think afresh about what we want and ought to be able to expect of our government.

# Acknowledgments

THIS BOOK COULD NOT HAVE BEEN WRITTEN without the help and support of many caring people, both professional colleagues from my department, university, and other universities, and my family and personal friends. Among my professional colleagues are Thomas J. Volgy, whose valued friendship and professional advice I am extremely fortunate to have; Chuck Britton, John Buehler, Phil Chapman, Les Dunbar, Reid Ewing, Ken Godwin, Don Heckerman, Jim Hepworth, John Hollowell, Helen Ingram, Henry Kenski, Ron Oaxaca, Larry Scaff, Mike Sullivan, Gerry Swanson, and Shiela Tobias. Working with these generous and talented people in fields spanning the social sciences and humanities has been a singularly rewarding experience for me. I owe thanks also to Dorotha Bradley, Su-ming Lin, Anne Scott, and Ali Abootalebi, students at the University of Arizona who encouraged the writing of the book and spent many hard hours helping me to check the factual material contained in it. No one contributed more to the birth of the book than did Mary Sue

## Acknowledgments

McQuown, whose secretarial assistance was invaluable and whose advice constantly helped me to see what I had not seen before. I am appreciative of the help given by Kelli Waldron, too. Among members of my family and my personal friends, I am heavily indebted to David and Morris Lasker, Peggy Akin, James Bendix, Lonny Baker, Chris Heflin, Eilene Hollowell, and Cindy Resnick, each of whom was there when it was crucial. I am grateful also to George P. Brockway and Roby Harrington, and to the many others at W.W. Norton who have worked on the book. Finally, to my parents and the four to whom this book is dedicated goes my heartfelt appreciation for their continuing encouragement and for everything that they have given me.

All of these people made substantial contributions to the pages that follow. I deeply thank each and every one of them. Any shortcomings that remain are solely the responsibility of the author.

# AMERICA'S HIDDEN SUCCESS

## REVISED

# 1

## The Decline of Confidence in Government

DURING THE 1980s a new legacy came into being in America. Advocating the values of individual freedom and self-reliance, and championing reduced governmental interference in economic and social affairs, the Reagan administration moved energetically to change the course of public policy in the United States. Following a dramatic rise in government spending on social programs from 1960 to 1980, budget priorities shifted away from these aims in the Reagan years. Taxes on individuals and corporations were cut in the attempt to restore incentive and revive a stalled economy. Some of the key regulatory activities of government, considered to have ensnarled free enterprise, were streamlined or ended altogether.

The new direction of thinking that underlay these policies constituted a reversal of the political ideology that had guided the nation for the prior fifty years, under both Democratic and Republican administrations. For two full generations after 1932 the view prevailed in America that government could be used successfully as an instrument to achieve the public good. Americans believed that their government, through thoughtfully orchestrated programs, could help build a more decent and just life for all amid a prosperous, growing economy. This belief provided the foundation for the New Deal, the Fair Deal, the New Frontier, and the Great Society, programs spanning presidents from Franklin Roosevelt to Lyndon Johnson, and also permeated many of the domestic policies of the Nixon, Ford, and Carter administrations. Every year throughout this fifty-year period, seemingly, new governmental programs were formulated and new kinds of governmental assistance and regulation devised.

Shadows of doubt about this philosophy lengthened during the two decades of the post-Eisenhower era, the years from 1960 to 1980. In these twenty years disillusionment with the economic and social policies of the nation increasingly spread.[1] Everything, it appeared, had turned sour. A whole litany of problems arose. By the mid-1970s the real incomes of American families had stopped growing. Each month, it seemed, inflation rose and unemployment lines swelled. The nation's industrial engine appeared to be worn, incapable of creating needed new jobs. Meanwhile, governmental spending increased year after year, its programs growing more costly yet apparently accomplishing few positive results. With each passing year the government's tax bite became ever larger, yet revenues never sufficed to pay the government's bills. By 1978 popular disenchantment had reached groundswell proportions. A series of tax revolts, starting with Proposition 13 in California, swept through states and cities all across the nation.

Out of this wave of disillusionment arose the outlook that would dominate the 1980s. With ringing phrases and compelling rhetoric, Ronald Reagan expressed more powerfully than anyone else the profound disenchantment with government that many Americans felt. He believed that government had not only failed to solve America's problems, but had become the problem itself.[2] Consider the government's antipoverty programs. By 1980 growing percentages of Americans, believing that these programs had become both too costly and counterproductive, wanted to cut back the aid to the poor.[3] President Reagan became the spokesman for this view. The expansion of these programs during and after President Johnson's Great Society, Reagan claimed, had resulted in a "long and sorry tale of disappointment." The Great Society had hurt, not helped. After the increase in public assistance, the president said, "poverty stopped shrinking and actually began to grow worse . . . leaving millions of Americans trapped in a cycle of welfare dependency."[4]

Just as the government's antipoverty programs had proved counterproductive for the poor and led to handouts, so the incessant growth of governmental spending, taxation, and regulation had placed heavy burdens on the economy, sapping it of its strength, and leading inevitably to the spread of unemployment and the rise of inflation. The economy's downward spiral seemed to gather momentum as the decade of the 1970s advanced. The decline of America's economy, the president told the nation, resulted from "these last few decades [of] increased intervention by the government in the marketplace, tax policies that took too great a percentage of overall earnings, plus burdensome and unnecessary regulations."[5]

Many of the ills besetting the nation, the president believed, sprang from the wild growth and mismanagement of government. His repeated allusions to badly conceived governmental policies, unbridled governmental growth, and a faltering economy merely recalled the images almost all Americans had, and still have in one fashion or another, about the record of the post-Eisenhower years from 1960 to 1980. The election and reelection of President Reagan in 1980 and 1984 as well as the enactment and implementation of much of his policy agenda were the natural consequences of these images of failure.

The political pressures that these images of failure unleashed were so powerful indeed that governmental policy began to shift away from the existing policies several years prior to the 1980 election, during the Carter presidency.[6] After President Reagan's election, too, the images of past failure continued to cow the Democrats, with the result that the president's domination over the debate remained nearly complete. Broadly accepting the critique of government, the Democrats rarely set forth new proposals that espoused governmental activism. Even today the foundation of political debate in America rests on the basic agreement by all parties—although to somewhat different degrees, to be sure—that the post-Eisenhower years were a disappointing failure in the economic and social realms and that mismanagement by government played a major role.

Nevertheless, in spite of President Reagan's immense talent for communication and the vivid stories describing failed government that he brought before the public, Americans did not accept his view *in toto.* True, the generally negative attitudes of Americans toward government closely mirrored the beliefs of the president. On the other hand, public demand for governmental services in numerous specific areas remained strong. For example, majorities of Americans have wanted government to do more to help the elderly and, in certain respects, even the poor, to improve environmental quality, and to protect consumers and enhance the safety of workers.[7] Thus the present values that call for reduced governmental interference still compete with the values of the past that call for governmental activism, sometimes coming into conflict even within the same individuals.

The contradiction here is often between the general and the specific—the general doubts that most Americans have today about the efficacy of action through government against the sense most Americans have that more governmental action is needed in many specific areas. If we are to resolve this fundamental contradiction in the views of Americans, a crucial question needs answering. Our negative attitudes about government have been informed by the images of the failure

5

of governmental activism in the past. Yet are these images valid? In order to come to grips with the choices facing us in the present, we need to reinvestigate the legacy of failure of the past.

## Individual Lives

Articulating the case against governmental activism, the critics of government, such as President Reagan, allude to an array of individual illustrations of welfare cheats and bureaucratic waste and ineptitude: the welfare recipient who lives in a swanky hotel room, permitted to live off public assistance rather than getting a job and working; the man who pays his bill at the supermarket with food stamps and then drives off in a Cadillac; the small entrepreneur rendered unable to make his business work successfully by a maze of governmental regulations that have built up during the half century since the New Deal.

Yet powerful examples also exist on the other side of the ledger. Use of individual instances to criticize governmental policies, while having been potent, fails to consider the ways in which government has touched people in a positive direction. One of the first people to use the War on Poverty was a 22-year-old woman named Ernestine, a Hispanic mother from a small New Mexico farming town. Herself a high school dropout, she decided in 1966 to enter her child into the local Head Start program for low-income children at a nearby elementary school. So that she would be able to assist her child, Ernestine received educational training toward her high school degree under the auspices of

6

Head Start. She completed high school and, with the government's assistance once more, went on to college. Then, after graduating college, she continued in school earning first one and eventually a second master's degree. Today, Ernestine is the principal of the elementary school her child entered nearly twenty years ago as a Head Start student.

Illustrations of the positive role government has played in the lives of Americans are by no means rare. President Reagan has himself known many such people, some his entire lifetime. Consider the president's own father, Jack Reagan.[8] While living in Dixon, Illinois, he lost his job on Christmas Eve of 1931 in the midst of the depression. Unable to locate other permanent work, he also proved unsuccessful in realizing his lifelong dream of a partnership in a shoe shop. Eventually, in early 1933, he was rescued from the depression not by the private sector, but instead through the government's help. He got a job in the local welfare office and then, shortly thereafter, was put in charge of the local Works Progress Administration (WPA), which created public jobs for the unemployed. Nor was he the only family member to do so. Soon after the depression closed his plant in 1933, the president's brother, Neil, also got a job through the WPA.

Even the people whom President Reagan brings to public attention as examples of the American dream frequently have a side to their lives which contradicts the president's theme. When the Chicago Bears' Walter Payton became the leading rusher in the history of the National Football League several years ago, the president spoke to him over nationwide television. Here was a true American hero, stirring testimony to what the individual could accomplish in America by sheer hard work and the determination and will to succeed. Nevertheless, unbeknownst to most, the American government had played a crucial role in Walter Payton's life. When Payton was growing up in Columbia, Mississippi, he became the first black ever to play on his high school team, able to do so because of the government's firm insistence on civil rights and racial integration in schools.[9] In fact, even as the president lauded this American hero, his own administration was simultaneously trying to pull back federal efforts in civil rights by way of a policy that would grant federal funding to colleges and tax-exempt status to private schools without regard to whether they sponsored programs that discriminated against minorities and women.

Another hero, one of considerable personal significance to President Reagan, is Dr. Joseph Giordano, the surgeon who attended the president after the assassination attempt on his life in 1981. The president, while praising Dr. Giordano before a national conference of Italian-Americans, related that Dr. Giordano was the son of a milkman whose own family had been impoverished immigrants. Through his own and his parents' hard work, the president continued, Dr. Giordano had risen to enter college and then medical school on his way to becoming a surgeon and eventually to saving the life of a president.[10] All this was true, yet Dr. Giordano explains his rise to success in different terms. He observes: "The government social programs enacted over

8

the last 50 years—and so frequently criticized by this President and his Administration—have played a vital role in making this success possible."[11] The president was perhaps unaware that Dr. Giordano had completed medical school with the assistance of low-interest federal educational loans, and that his parents have been helped by governmental programs, too. "In contrast to the President, who feels that government programs make people so dependent that they lose initiative," Dr. Giordano said, "I feel that these programs have enabled people with little resources to reach their full potential."[12]

## Components of Good Government

These examples highlight the beneficial role that government can play in the lives of individuals. Yet examples of this nature do not provide the sort of systematic evidence that demonstrates, one way or the other, whether governmental programs go further than helping isolated individuals also to serve the public good. The problem with examples is just that: they are individual instances and can be used to argue all sides of the issue. How, then, can one decide the basic question: has governmental activism ably served the public or has it instead failed?

There are certain criteria used to assess public programs, formally by specialists in public policy, intuitively by citizens and taxpayers. These criteria include: effectiveness—whether governmental programs deal with problems better than could be accomplished by private action, and whether they do so without causing negative side effects; second, efficiency—whether the programs are affordable, and whether they are the least costly alternatives toward fixing the problems; and, third, representativeness—whether the programs accord with mainstream Americans' attitudes and beliefs about how current problems should be resolved.

From the standpoint of these criteria, it is certainly reasonable to ask, as Americans do, that governmental programs be effective: that the programs produce discernibly better results than could be achieved through private action. A part of this is the expectation that the programs—however well they alleviate the problems they are designed to tackle—not be counterproductive. For example, a policy that attempts to reduce poverty is patently ineffective if it fails to reduce poverty. However, it is also ineffective if the policy reduces the numbers in poverty and the worst effects of poverty, but only by making the poor dependent upon public assistance when they could, by working, lift themselves out of poverty. Such a policy clearly won't do. Nor will an antipoverty policy whose need for resources burdens the economy, thereby resulting in the creation of fewer jobs and less opportunity for the poor. An "effective" policy to reduce poverty, then, must show that it reduces the number of poor without producing countervailing side effects. Yet, as the years from 1960 to 1980 advanced, the public perceived that the proliferation and expansion of social programs led to both welfare dependency and a worsened economy and job picture. This perception caused growing numbers of voters and political officials to support trimming back the government's role.

Apart from effectiveness, questions were also raised about the efficiency of actions undertaken by the government. Efficiency has two aspects to it. At a minimum, the cost of government must remain affordable to the taxpayer. But, even if affordable, the particular programs chosen must be relatively inexpensive. That is, there should be no other discernibly less costly means available—whether public or private—by which the same or similar ends of policy can be accomplished. Further, the implementation of the programs should be carried out with little waste and fraud. The popular view went otherwise, however. It became commonplace after 1965 to believe that the costs of government had spiraled dangerously and that cheaper means were available. Powered by this belief, and coupled with a nearly endless number of stories of waste, fraud, and extravagant spending within the government's programs, disillusionment of the American public with government grew widespread over the years following 1960.

As the post-Eisenhower era advanced, critics of the policies of the era sometimes also claimed to represent a "silent majority" from which the government had grown distant. This suggests the use of a third criterion in making assessments about good government. Put simply, governmental policies ought to be reflective of public views. Even had governmental programs been effective and efficient, it would matter little if, in the process, those policies had substantially diverged from the sentiments and concerns of the public. The public's perception, according to public opinion polls taken from 1960 to 1980, was that government increasingly failed to listen to Americans.[13]

For one thing, the critics claimed that Americans had a differing set of priorities for government. Crime and urban turmoil headed up the list of concerns, they claimed, not poverty, discrimination, and pollution. For another, there was the matter of approach: Did the public truly want a multitude of different programs for the poor in preference to a single, more comprehensive system of guaranteed income, for example? To clean up the environment, did Americans really desire a series of regulatory programs leading to higher prices in preference to a more direct system of governmental grants to businesses? Only if government reflected popular views both about the priority that individual issues should be given and about the approach considered most desirable to the solution of those issues could the government be described as representative of the American public.[14]

That the government be effective, efficient, and representative of the public view are three tough but ultimately just and reasonable criteria to ask good government to meet. How well did America's government fare according to these criteria? The record compiled by government, first at its most active from 1960 to 1980 and then at a more modest level in the years thereafter, tells a story far removed from the conventional wisdom. It is a story of realities that have thus far been well hidden from view.

In Chapters 2 through 5 the government's actions and record during the twenty years leading up to the Reagan election are explored in a variety of areas spanning poverty, the environment, and the economy. These chapters discuss the performance of the 1960–80 years measured against the sharpest and most compelling criticisms that have been raised against the practice of affirmative government, the same criticisms upon which the new conservative direction of policy rode to power in the 1980s. These chapters also consider how the negative attitudes about government during the post-Eisenhower years arose. Chapter 6 then takes the story a step further. It directly compares the record of the post-Eisenhower era from 1960 to 1980 with the performance of the policies of the years that followed. Simultaneously, it answers the argument and evidence found in the strongest and most highly publicized critique of affirmative government to appear in the Reagan era, that of Charles Murray's *Losing Ground.*[15] Finally, the epilogue takes the concluding step. It builds upon a more realistic assessment of government from 1960 to the present to offer guidelines for more productive policies for America in the future.

## The Setting

To gain a true measure of the performance of America's government and economy in the years after 1960, it is necessary at the outset to understand the context. The perceptions of failure that came to permeate the Americans' views did not arise out of thin air. They were not simply the fabrication of forces hostile to affirmative government.

There were many developments suggesting, for instance, that by the 1970s America's economy had spun into decline. For one, America's international balance of payments became negative in the 1970s for the first time since World War II. Even more important, some of the most crucial indicators that directly touched Americans' pocketbooks suggested the same. For much of the 1970s neither wages nor family income increased after adjusting for inflation. Unemployment rose by nearly 3 million workers in the single decade. Disturbing developments, they followed more than two decades in which after-inflation wages and incomes had advanced faster than ever before in American history. The nation was coming off a high, but in the 1970s economic progress seemed not merely to have slowed down; it appeared to have stopped dead in its tracks.

The symptoms of illness and decline were there, and so was economic hardship as the nation approached the 1980s. Yet symptoms can also be misleading if not understood in their proper context. Consider the following example. Compare the symptoms of a person who is experiencing heart failure with those of another person, a fit weight lifter who is in the process of lifting several hundred pounds. These two people are in the opposite states of health. Yet, despite different conditions of health, both people exhibit many of the same outward symptoms: reddish skin coloration, heavy breathing and perspiration, abnormal heart rate, and unusual fatigue. Similar symptoms can coincide with very different states of health.

Although most Americans never understood it this way, the economy of the United States was engaged in the equivalent of a strenuous weight lift throughout most of the years from 1960 to 1980. A net addition of 30 million workers entered the work force from the postwar baby boom generation, overwhelming the American labor market from 1964 to 1980. Whereas virtually the same number of Americans aged 16–35 were working in 1964 (27.4 million) as had been in 1947 (27.1 million), that figure skyrocketed from 27 million to 54 million between 1964 and 1980.[16] To complicate matters, the economy was forced to carry a second heavy burden. As the economy attempted somehow to lift this tidal wave of more than 50 million baby boomers into jobs, it simultaneously had to confront and overcome two giant increases in world energy prices in the period from 1973 through 1980. After the mid-1960s, these dramatic developments set the context in which the domestic policies of government had to operate. They also gave birth to the symptoms that Americans mistook for disease.

To illustrate, an economy whose strong growth from 1945 to 1965 had been able to translate into advancing wages now had to be redirected into the rapid generation of new jobs that would replace wage hikes in the effort to absorb the net addition of 30 million new workers. Even then some growth of unemployment was likely. The economy could demonstrate the same vitality and grow as powerfully as before, but the symptoms of disease and decline (stagnancy in after-inflation income and a rise of unemployment, which was popularly called "stagflation") would nevertheless emerge. They would be an outgrowth of the far weightier burdens that the economy had to carry. In the end, the public saw the symptoms with great clarity but never clearly understood the origins of the heavier burdens. Americans knew that something was weighing the economy down, all right. However, at a time when confidence in government was already at a low in the wake of Vietnam and Watergate, the public easily came to believe during the 1970s, along with many political leaders, that the heavier burdens draining the economy's vitality arose from the government itself and its alleged growth and mismanagement of domestic policy. Confusing the symptoms of disease for the illness itself, and disturbed by the economy's apparently unyielding problems, the public elected President Reagan, who placed the blame on government and promised to reverse the trend toward governmental activism that America had followed for a half century.

# 2

---

# Politics and Performance from 1960 to 1980: How Much Did Progress Follow Promise?

THE IDEA OF A STRONG, active government became an accepted value in American culture about half a century ago. The decisive turn of events occurred, of course, in the early 1930s when the private economy proved inadequate to the task of lifting the nation out of economic depression. More recently, the possible usefulness of the government rose to national attention in still many other areas. By the end of the 1950s, it appeared unlikely that the private sector would substantially lessen racial discrimination without governmental intervention. Nor could the private sector seem to do enough to mitigate the conditions of poverty that engulfed the lives of one in five American families even as Eisenhower left office. In the late 1960s, the problems of protecting the environment from pollution, consumers from unsafe products, and employees from dangerous workplaces were added to the lengthening list of con-

17

cerns for which governmental action seemed a necessary solution. With the broad backing of the American public, the government confronted each of these and many other far-reaching issues. The belief that the government could help build a more decent society flourished during these years.

As the nation entered the 1980s, however, an entirely different mood prevailed. Dramatic changes in the nation's fortunes had taken place, changes that increasingly undermined the confidence in government that had arisen out of the depression and the decades that followed. With the advance of the post-Eisenhower years, for a multiplicity of reasons, the government's programs no longer appeared to work successfully, and the government was widely perceived to have been more incompetent than competent in addressing a wide range of issues. Governmental programs treating the economic and social problems of the day began to impress many Americans as ineffectual, possibly even compounding the existing problems as much as resolving them. Not surprisingly, by 1980 the number of Americans embracing the belief that "government is run by people who don't know what they're doing" climbed to a solid 63 percent, up from 27 percent in the first half of the 1960s.[1] The feeling was widespread that the government was wasting large amounts of the public's money: In 1980 almost four in five Americans held this opinion, compared with fewer than half of us twenty years earlier.

The view taken by conservatives broadly mirrored the nation's sharp change in attitude toward governmental matters. Since conservatives felt that the fault with government lay partly in its having attempted too much, they proposed a simple, clear solution: The government would do better to assume a more diminished role.[2] Believing that the government's programs had often been ineffective in dealing with the nation's problems, many conservative leaders claimed that once the excessive burdens of governmental intervention were removed, the private-enterprise system could generate a level of prosperity that would help those millions of distressed Americans whom the government's programs had allegedly failed.[3] Against the background of two decades of mounting skepticism about the government, this argument succeeded in becoming enormously attractive, eventually transforming both the politics and public policies of the time.

If we are to understand our present position, we must resolve the myriad of misgivings that arose during the post-Eisenhower era about the domestic programs of government, programs that played a major part in the nation's life. After 1960, governmental action expanded very rapidly on a variety of domestic fronts. Two crucial priorities of these years were the alleviation of poverty and the control of environmental pollution. In the attempt to meet these objectives, a multiplicity of programs arose or were vastly expanded almost overnight, programs that demanded the largest increases of the post-Eisenhower era in the spending of tax money and the use of governmental regulatory power. Precisely because of the tens of billions of dollars the government spent on these large programs and the power

19

it wielded, very basic questions have to be asked—and answered. Did these programs serve the nation well? What of real value did all the effort and money accomplish? Indeed, was governmental involvement on such a massive scale even necessary? Was it correct to have considered that the private sector could not be utilized to a much greater effect in these spheres, or that perhaps some other type of scaled-down governmental action could not be made more effective? Did the government run the programs of the post-Eisenhower years in a manner that avoided great amounts of waste? Our largely negative answers to these questions rightly haunt us, for they lead to conclusions that have contributed decisively to the severe judgment we have made about the recent past and about the role of our government in creating that past.

That those who advocated a more active government, in what now seems the distant past, showed far greater insight into the challenges that beset the nation is little recognized by many Americans today. There is a critical lesson for us to learn about the post-Eisenhower years, a lesson that was clear to many of those advocates of a stronger government. This lesson teaches us that whatever good results a prosperous private sector and a growing economy realized during these years— and the economy of the post-Eisenhower years did grow fantastically—they did not address the two main priorities of the time: the reduction of poverty and the control of environmental pollution. Only through the government and the government's programs could the nation penetrate the surface of either of these complex problems. To the degree that we fail to come to grips with this lesson, we will likely pay a substantial price, an important element of which will be our continued mistaken impression that somehow we took the wrong road in our immediate past.

## Poverty in America

Scenes from the winter of 1960–61:

A 33-year-old man known to our agency was found hanged in his apartment just seven hours ago. He was apparently despondent over not being able to find a job, and unemployment compensation had been exhausted. His wife and four children had left him and had returned to Mississippi where they had immigrated from seven years ago. The family had been several months [in] arrears in rent, and there was not proper food and clothing for the family during the harsh Chicago winter months.[4]

A man over the age of forty has been in search of a job for eighteen months: "When I come to the hiring window, the man just looks at me; he doesn't even ask questions; he says, 'You're too old.' "[5]

She gently wept as she told me of her small daughter: "I can remember just like it was yesterday at the hospital with my Lisa. We didn't eat much in those days. Maybe we'd have potatoes and bread is all, or beans. We had one room and it was always cold and damp. A lot of sickness, too. This time Lisa was sick, so sick I didn't know what to do her fever was so high. Scared is what I was. I went down to the hospital carrying her in my arms. I had no doctor, no money. I sat the whole day through in the hospital rocking her. The whole day just waiting to see a doctor until my Lisa died right in my arms.[6]

Because the percentage of people living below the poverty line in the United States remained substantial even at the end of the 1950s, the attempt to reduce poverty in America was no small undertaking at the start of the post-Eisenhower years.[7] In the wealthiest nation ever at the beginning of the 1960s about one in every five of us lived in a condition of poverty.[8] Flagrant malnutrition, substandard housing, and pitifully inadequate medical care were common.

Consider this. Imagine all the people living today in the industrial states of Massachusetts and Michigan, with such cities as Boston and Detroit. Then add all the people living in the states of Minnesota, Colorado, Oregon, Arizona, Maryland, and Kentucky. These states contain Minneapolis, St. Paul, Denver, Portland, Phoenix, Tucson, Baltimore, and Louisville. To complete the picture, include some of the more rural states such as New Hampshire, South Carolina, and Iowa. Then imagine every person in every one of these states living in poverty. That describes the number of people and the breadth of the poverty existing in America in 1960 at the end of the Eisenhower era.

Another point must be understood. Many Americans living in poverty either had jobs or had worked for their entire adult life. During the early 1960s, the heads of about half the families living in poverty held jobs, and one out of every four impoverished family heads had full-time employment all year long. Even in the last half of the 1970s, about 1 million heads of poor families in America who were employed full time were still living below the poverty line.[9] They and their dependents numbered almost 5 million Americans. The size of the problem is made real enough by these figures. As head of a family of four, could a worker earn his or her way out of poverty? Possibly, but for many Americans—bookkeepers, laborers, janitors, secretaries, household workers, library aides, small farmers, cashiers, receptionists, nurse's aides—not easily.

With poverty facing from 30 million to 40 million Americans in 1960, and near-poverty facing millions more, the government created or greatly enlarged many programs during the ensuing Kennedy, Johnson, and Nixon years. These programs can be divided into at least three general categories. First, some programs gave direct aid in the form of income, which recipients could use for any purpose. Among the well-known examples are Aid to Families with Dependent Children, supplemental income programs for the impoverished elderly, social security, and unemployment compensation. A second kind of program worked toward a more specific end. It was intended to assure that certain basic needs would be met, particularly the nutritional, medical, and housing needs of impoverished persons as well as other categories of persons covered under the programs. The best known among these programs are Medicare and Medicaid, food stamps, and the public housing and rent supplement programs. The third type of program had quite a different objective. It sought to improve the skills of impoverished or near-impoverished persons to enable them to become independent, and thus to compete and earn a secure living in the private economy. Examples of these programs are Head

Start and the job training and job creation programs.

Toward the end of the 1960s, a view emerged that suggested that these social programs had been expanded far more than Americans wanted and that the programs had become more creatures of the government than the expression of the public. This idea took many forms. Most memorable were the repeated references to the existence of a "silent majority" of Americans whose attitudes were very different from those expressed in the domestic goals and programs of the government. However, evidence from a succession of public-opinion polls indicates that a solid majority of Americans backed the government's effort to reduce poverty from the start and continued to do so throughout and even beyond the period during which the programs had become fully established. In acting to eliminate poverty and in greatly enlarging the programs, the government traveled down paths that virtually all segments of the American public warmly approved.[10]

## The Results of the Attack on Poverty

Perhaps the best overall indicator of the substantial progress made by the nation in the battle against poverty after 1960 is that by the second half of the 1970s only 4 to 8 percent of the American public remained beneath the poverty level compared with about 18 percent in 1960.[11] These figures take into account the income Americans received from every source, including income from all private economic activities and the private sector as well as from governmental programs. In the space of one generation, the economic growth of the times combined with the government's programs had reduced poverty among Americans by about 60 percent.

To what extent did this accomplishment owe itself to the government's programs as contrasted to the extraordinary expansion of the nation's economy over much of the period? To many, the answer is obvious. Probably most would agree with Martin Anderson, formerly President Reagan's chief domestic aide, who emphasizes the growing economy. In his view the most important single force was "the strong, sustained economic growth of the private sector."[12] This answer is so obvious to Anderson that he feels little need to offer much evidence in its defense. He simply points to the vigorous economic growth that took place in the nation during the 1960s and early 1970s: the enormous expansion of real national income as well as of wages and salaries and the spectacular growth in new jobs that occurred over these years.[13] From this it follows, presumably, that poverty would also be greatly reduced. True, the private sector provided 83 percent of all employment during the post-Eisenhower years. Considering the sheer magnitude of the private sector, perhaps it is only natural to infer that the economic growth of the private sector was a prime factor in the reduction of poverty in America.

This common presumption, however, is in error. Rather, the reduction of poverty was accomplished primarily through the government's programs. Anderson is correct in stating that real economic growth mushroomed from 1960 to 1980. To appreciate the government's contribution to the reduction of poverty, we can look at the decline in poverty during a period of vigorous economic expansion at the midpoint of the post-Eisenhower years. From 1965 through 1972, the real, disposable income per American rose, on an average, about 3 percent per year, or 24 percent over the seven years.[14] Because I am speaking of real, disposable income, this 24 percent growth is what remained in our pockets *after* subtracting for inflation and most taxes that we paid to the government. More growth in real, disposable income per American occurred in the seven years from 1965 to the end of 1972 than took place during the entire decade of the glorious 1950s, when income per person climbed by about 13 percent. The gross national product also rose at a faster annual rate between 1965 and 1972 than it had during the 1950s.

Surely one would anticipate that a period of such robust economic growth—growth that was very strong after inflation and taxes—would lower the percentage of impoverished Americans. The validity of this presumption can be examined by considering what the private economy accomplished in reducing poverty. Let us compare 1965 and 1972. When one takes all income except that transferred to individuals through governmental programs, census evidence for 1965 indicates that about 21.3 percent of the public would have been living in poverty; in 1972, again considering all sources of income except that received from governmental programs, census figures show that about 19.2 percent of the public would have been living in poverty, about one-tenth less than in 1965.[15] Thus, the private sector, in these times of substantial economic growth, reduced the percentage of Americans living in poverty by about one in every ten Americans; and exclusive of governmental programs, even by 1972 almost one in five Americans would still have been living in poverty.

Obviously, the economy's growth during these highly prosperous years alleviated poverty only marginally. In contrast to private economic performance, consider the performance of the programs of government. As a result of the government's programs, more than half of the remaining 19 percent of impoverished Americans rose above the poverty line, leaving about 9 percent of the American people below the poverty line by 1972; and by the late 1970s that figure was further reduced to between 7 and 8 percent, and possibly even lower.[16]

But how could this be? Why did vigorous economic growth on its own make such little headway in reducing poverty among Americans? Why were governmental programs necessary? The experience of the 1960s and early 1970s reveals fissures in the theory that poverty will necessarily be reduced by a robustly growing economy. For in certain crucial circumstances, economic growth does not help the very weak. Several major groups of Americans—groups that comprised millions upon millions of people across the nation—were almost completely excluded from the benefits of the private economic growth that occurred over these years.

The expanding economy did not directly touch, at least not very much, the impoverished elderly, for example. Most of our elderly are retired. Senior citizens who try to find jobs after retirement soon learn—if they can locate new employment at all—that the private sector is often unwilling to pay more than a marginal wage to people over 65 who reenter the labor market. This reality becomes ever more omnipresent when the labor markets are overcrowded with job seekers and the competition for jobs is intense, a circumstance that prevailed during the entire 1965–80 period with the maturation of the children of the postwar "baby boom" and the increased number of women taking up employment due to a change in attitude about entering the work force and necessity engendered by the rising incidence of marital separation and divorce.[17] Although the private economy grew markedly in the second half of the 1960s and early 1970s, it hardly touched the poverty level of the elderly at all, male or female.[18] Real, disposable income per person rose by about 24 percent during the 1965–72 period in the nation as a whole; yet, outside the effects of the government's programs, the percentage of male-headed elderly families below the poverty line declined by only 6 percent, from 57 to 51 percent. For female-headed elderly families, the percentage remained at 45 both in 1965 and 1972, amounting to no reduction in poverty at all among these families outside the functioning of the government's programs. Thus, a prosperously growing economy in the nation at large did little, directly, for the impoverished elderly.

A second important group of Americans bypassed by the expanding economy included white and nonwhite families headed by women under the age of 65. Although more than one in seven families are headed by women, the average earnings of women in the private economy are about 60 percent that of males. In addition, the jobs available to women are often dead end, with little possibility for advancement. Again, when the labor markets teem and the competition for jobs is severe, opportunities for women are particularly limited. In this light, consider the plight of white female family heads under the age of 65. The period from 1965 through 1972 produced a remarkable result with respect to this group. Exclusive of the government's programs, a slightly *higher* proportion of these female-headed families found themselves in poverty in 1972 than in 1965: Forty percent of these families lived in poverty in 1972, an increase of 4 percent over 1965.[19] And the figures for nonwhite female family heads under the age of 65 are no more encouraging. The nation's substantial economic growth made little dent in the levels of poverty experienced by these families, for, aside from the government's programs, poverty within this group dropped only 3 percent, from 69 percent in 1965 to 66 percent in 1972.[20]

The situation encountered by women in the private sector of the economy has always been difficult. Even after very high rates of growth, the private economy left millions of women and their families in poverty, as great a percentage after the economic expansion as before. Traditionally, the job opportunities available to women have been more marginal than those available to men, and in the crowded labor markets of the post-Eisenhower years, the competition women faced in getting better jobs only increased in intensity as compared with earlier years. In addition, as family separations grew in numbers, more and more single women were required to assume the role of family head. Employment opportunities for women with very young children to care for are indeed scarce. This combination of very difficult circumstances helps explain what the census figures on poverty show: Had it not been for the government's presence, hardly any change in the rate of poverty facing this very large group of Americans would have been realized over the whole of this prosperous period.

The plight of a third group, really a subgroup of females, the families headed by females under the age of 25, is similarly desperate. For the young, who are just beginning their work careers, are highly vulnerable in a labor market full to overflowing and an economy undergoing change. The rate of poverty among these families in 1965 was 62 percent; by 1972, although personal income growth in real terms had risen by more than one-fifth per American in the nation at large, the percentage of these families living beneath the poverty level remained the same.[21] Seven years of vigorous economic growth had not alleviated their situation by even one percentage point.

On its own, above-average economic expansion reduced the overall rate of poverty among American people marginally, from 21.3 percent (exclusive of governmental programs) in 1965 to 19.2 percent in 1972. Whereas economic growth reduced the poverty of one in ten Americans, governmental intervention reduced that of more than one in two Americans over the same period, a rate five to six times greater than that of the private economy. Economic growth did help some segments of the population, particularly families headed by males (white and nonwhite) under the age of 65. Among these families, rates of poverty declined sharply, by one-third or more, exclusive of governmental intervention.[22] Yet, these were the strongest and most competitive economic groups, groups that entered the era of economic expansion already with, comparatively, the lowest rates of poverty. By way of contrast, economic expansion made little or no difference to the poverty rates of many other groups, particularly the elderly, white and minority women, and the youngest of the economically weak. In light of this experience, it would be nothing less than blind faith to argue that vigorous economic growth alone would have effectively reduced poverty in America within a reasonable time span. The circumstances of the 1960s and early 1970s demonstrate that while a prosperous economy may benefit the stronger economic groups, its impact on weaker groups can equally be nonexistent, reducing some to even more dire situations. *The government's programs were vital in fighting poverty precisely because the private sector was itself incapable of making more than a marginal dent in poverty among the many millions of Americans who remained trapped within the weaker economic groups,* either too old to get work or channeled into dead-end jobs that often paid little more than half-time wages for full-time work. Including their dependents, more than 30 million Americans lived in such families.

The economic experience of the 1960s and 1970s equally belies a second familiar belief, that is, that wel-

31

fare programs substantially reduce the incentive to work. True, some effect is possible; it is most likely to be experienced by those Americans who remain at or near the poverty level even when holding down full-time jobs. Nevertheless, neither the expansion of the poverty programs in the 1960s and 1970s, nor the decisive contribution they made to reducing poverty, seems to have come at the cost of much reduction in the incentive of Americans to become a part of the work force and earn a living. To help set the context, consider that the numbers of people seeking work and taking jobs increased at historically high rates during these years, by 35 percent in 1965–80 alone. Employment climbed at a far faster pace during and after the great acceleration of the poverty and welfare programs in 1965–80 than during the preceding fifteen-year period (employment during 1950–65 rose by 21 percent). How much more might employment have climbed had there been less spending on welfare? One estimate of the impact of welfare programs on employment brings together the results of a host of other studies. It suggests that had all the main public-assistance programs for persons under the age of 65 been completely eliminated, including Aid to Families with Dependent Children, Medicaid, food stamps, and veterans' benefits, the numbers of hours worked by Americans would have risen by about 1 percent.[23] Another point, too, helps place matters in perspective: Following 1965, even as the government's poverty and welfare programs experienced their most rapid enlargement, the rate of increase in unemployment in the United States rose *less* than it did in most other major Western nations.[24] The vast expansion in the number of employed people after 1965, an increase diminished hardly at all by the welfare programs, and the comparatively slow rate of growth in the nation's unemployment make it apparent that the expansion of the government's attempts to attack poverty had very little effect on the number of Americans with the desire and incentive to work.

If so many filled jobs, who then were the families living on welfare? The single, largest federal welfare program giving direct cash assistance to low-income Americans is Aid to Families with Dependent Children (AFDC). The AFDC population is distinguished by three main characteristics: the male- and the female-headed families are entirely different, the female-headed families are in the large majority, and most families remain on AFDC only a few years.

At the end of the 1970s, for example, the male-headed families constituted only about 14 percent of all families on the AFDC welfare rolls.[25] Of these, about half the family heads were incapacitated by injuries, black or brown lung disease, and other disabling physical handicaps and conditions.[26] Of the remaining male heads, most had no skills and had not completed high school.[27] By law, these able-bodied persons were required to participate in either a work-training program, about which more is said later, or the Work Incentive Program, a job location and placement service. Failure to cooperate in job placement under the Work Incentive Program could lead to the total loss of welfare assistance, a requirement that was likely used as much as a threat to gain compliance as in the final enforcement.

Throughout 1960–80, the large majority of AFDC families were headed by females.[28] Many of these family heads with very young children turned to AFDC when they were widowed or otherwise separated from their husbands.[29] Critics contend that long-term welfare dependency frequently develops in these families. However, because having very young children to care for is so often a crucial factor, and because the total number of children in AFDC families is small (just over two children per family on average), AFDC actually experiences a high turnover.[30] One study reports that 75 percent of all AFDC cases close within three years; another puts the figure at 60 percent.[31] Since participation in AFDC is commonly a relatively transitional experience, it becomes plausible that the most extensive exploration of family situations in America during the late 1960s and the 1970s would find *no* significant evidence that children from welfare families, compared with children from low-income families not on welfare, have themselves been disproportionately likely to go on welfare when they subsequently set up their own households.[32]

The work ethic continues to prevail in the United States. For the majority of AFDC recipients, the use of the federal government's major welfare program has been transitory, except when family heads are disabled. There exist few better indicators of the survival of the work ethic than to note the special kinds of situations that have commonly led families to turn to AFDC assistance and the relatively high turnover of the majority of families on welfare. Moreover, as a way of placing all this in context, it is relevant that even as such assistance became more widely available, the number of Americans who became employed grew at an unprecedented rate, one barely diminished by the programs' existence, and the rate of unemployment grew comparatively little. Even among the families living in poverty, the percentage of family heads who were employed in the late 1970s was almost as high as in the early 1960s, before the programs' rapid expansion.[33] The most powerful and widely cited critique of welfare, Charles Murray's *Losing Ground,* itself shows that welfare had little effect on unemployment.[34] Something else was going on in America; it was not a denial of the work ethic.

Instead, the economy's growth, combined with the sizable expansion of income after inflation that accompanied it, simply failed on its own to reach large numbers of people. As indicated earlier, this was due partly to the intensely crowded labor markets after 1965, a situation that will be described in detail in Chapter 4; here the important point concerns its decisive effect. The intense competition for jobs meant that, even though economic growth ran apace, an employer's market still prevailed, at times fabulously so, with the result that job seekers from the weaker economic groups were rendered even weaker. Despite these circumstances, the government programs of the post-Eisenhower era reduced the percentage of Americans living in poverty by more than half, greatly surpassing the impact of even a substantial expansion of the private economy, which itself reduced poverty by about 10 percent. Moreover, the private economy concentrated its smaller contribution on helping those Americans who were in the strongest economic position. The government's programs made their far larger contribution by reaching, and reducing poverty within, the economically less-competitive groups of American people, groups of Americans whose situations had generally been ignored by the vigorous expansion of the private sector.

## Nutrition, Health, and Housing

In addition to reducing poverty, another crucial goal of the attack on poverty was to raise the quality of people's lives, specifically with respect to essential human needs. Well into our times, devastating situations faced many low-income families in America concerning basic nutritional, health, and housing needs. To illustrate, just before the expansion of the governmental nutrition programs in the early 1970s, the Field Foundation undertook an investigation of the nutritional condition of Americans in impoverished locales. The foundation's report, prepared by a team of physicians, appeared in 1967, about the time of the Detroit riots. Its conclusions rocked the nation:

Wherever we went and wherever we looked, we saw children in significant numbers who were hungry and sick, children for whom hunger is a daily fact of life, and sickness, in many forms, an inevitability. [Many of these children] were hungry, weak, and apathetic. Their lives were being shortened . . . They were suffering from hunger and disease and, directly or indirectly, they were dying from them.[35]

This shattering picture is of the United States of America in 1967, less than one generation ago.

In response, the food-stamp program was expanded sharply, beginning in 1969, and the child nutrition programs also secured increased funding. The effect on the incidence of marginal malnutrition is uncertain, as few comprehensive nationwide figures exist. In view of the large expense of the programs, this represents a yawning gap in the evidence.[36] But in 1977 the Field Foundation team returned to the poverty-stricken areas of the Bronx, Appalachia, Mississippi, and Texas, which had been their laboratory a decade earlier. How much had things changed with the passage of the decade? Dr. Raymond Wheeler of the Charlotte Medical Center sums up what had happened in those ten years:

There can be little doubt that significant change has occurred since 1967. . . . Nowhere did I see the gross evidence of malnutrition among young children that we saw in 1967. . . . It is not possible any more to find very easily the bloated bellies, the shriveled infants, the gross evidence of vitamin and protein deficiencies in children that we identified in the late 1960s.[37]

The Field Foundation's observations suggest that the government's nutritional programs were almost fully effective in reducing flagrant malnutrition among Americans in locales of concentrated poverty across the nation, among both adults and children. It must be understood that 83 percent of the food-stamp benefits went to persons whose income would otherwise have fallen below the poverty level.[38] Dr. Gordon Harper, another member of the Field Foundation team, ob-

served that since 1967 there had been "a striking de-
crease in the number of grossly visible signs of malnutrition. Food stamps have made a critical difference."[39]

It is disturbing that wide sections of the public are
generally unaware of this improvement. It is an
achievement that should bring at least a degree of pride
in what the nation has done. But there is instead hardly
any sense of accomplishment, almost as if nothing at all
had taken place.

A similar conclusion pertains to the results of governmental programs in the medical sphere. In 1963, before
the implementation of Medicare and Medicaid, fully
one in five of those Americans living beneath the poverty level *had never been examined by a physician,* at
least not within their memory.[40] In many respects, use
of medical care was significantly lower among low-
income people as compared with middle- and high-
income groups, [41] despite the higher incidence of illness
and disease among impoverished persons.

Inequality describes the situation encountered by the
medical programs and the programs for the elderly that
were enacted in the middle of the 1960s. By 1970, only
five years later, notable changes had already taken
place, positive changes that were to continue into the
1970s. By 1970, the percentage of people living in poverty who had never visited a physician was reduced
from 19 percent in 1963 to 8 percent.[42] The percentage
of impoverished persons seeing a doctor at least once
a year approached that of high-income persons.[43] The
numbers of prenatal visits to physicians made by impoverished pregnant women rose dramatically.[44] Also,

the numbers of visits made to general physicians by impoverished persons increased. Reflecting the substantially higher rate of illness and disease among impoverished people, the number of visits to general physicians grew to average 4.9 a year per individual among impoverished persons by 1970, as compared with 3.8 visits a year per individual among middle- and high-income persons.[45]

Indeed, there can be little question that between 1963 and 1970 lower-income Americans gained increased access to medical care, an increase that is closely associated with the introduction of the federal medical programs.[46] The accomplishments of the nutritional and the medical components of the poverty programs were associated, in turn, with substantial improvements in the health of impoverished people.

The best single index of a community's general health is reputed to be its infant mortality rate. From 1965 to 1975, the overall infant mortality rate among the poor fell by fully 33 percent.[47] Gains among blacks were particularly evident. Between 1950 and 1965, before the great expansion in the federal medical and nutritional programs, the infant mortality rate among blacks barely fell, from 44.5 per 1,000 births in 1950 to 40.3 in 1965. Following the expansion of the programs, the rate of black infant mortality declined quickly, from 40.3 in 1965 to 30.9 in 1970, and to 24.2 in 1975.[48] There thus occurred about a fivefold increase in the speed of decline in the black infant mortality rate after 1965, a change about twice as pronounced as that occurring in the nonminority population. Other examples of the impact of poverty programs on the mortality rates among lower-income Americans abound. The infant mortality rates in some impoverished geographical areas were reduced by 50 percent within three to four years following the introduction of government-initiated nutritional and medical programs.[49]

Comparative figures are also available on this key indicator of a population's health. They, too, suggest an association between the enlargement of the government's programs and the rate of decline in the infant mortality rate. In 1965, prior to the expansion of the programs, thirteen nations across the globe, including West Germany, Great Britain, and the Soviet Union, experienced infant mortality rates similar to our own. The rate of decline in infant mortality in the United States from 1965 through 1975 exceeded those of all but four of the thirteen nations.[50] In achieving this result, the increase in health expenditures as a percentage of the GNP (from 5.2 percent in 1960 to 8.3 percent in 1975) grew little more in the United States than in other Western nations.[51]

Apart from the goal of improving nutritional and medical conditions, a third basic need governmental programs sought to serve centered on housing. Among the programs directed to basic needs, federal housing programs alone enjoy a continuous history, dating back to Arthurdale in 1933. By the 1970s about 3 million low-income families resided in housing subsidized partly or wholly by public funds. In addition, the government had long fostered a broader approach in the area of housing, an approach that employed tax incentives and guaranteed loans to stimulate the building and private purchase of new middle- and upper-income housing, thereby opening vacancies in existing housing for low-income buyers and renters. Tax relief for middle- and upper-income persons who purchase homes typically amounts to billions of dollars a year, and significant numbers of mortgage loans to purchase private homes are guaranteed by the government.

Clearly, these various governmental programs operated in conjunction with the private housing industry and the private housing market, in combination with increased real income, to affect housing conditions. Although the government played only a part, the combination of these forces accomplished much. In 1940, 20.2 percent of American households lived in overcrowded housing conditions (housing occupied by more than one person per room); twice as many, or 40 percent of black and other minority households, lived in overcrowded housing. Gradually, overcrowded housing has been reduced. In 1950, 16 percent of American households lived in overcrowded housing; by 1960 the figure was about 12 percent, by 1970 about 9 percent, and by 1976 less than 5 percent of all American households lived in overcrowded housing. The figure for black and minority families residing in overcrowded housing was reduced by more than 50 percent between 1940 and 1970.[52]

A similar reduction occurred in the percentage of Americans living in substandard housing. "Substandard" defines housing that lacks hot running water, or some or all other plumbing, or is in great physical disrepair. The percentage of American households living in such housing stood at almost 49 percent in 1940 and was slightly above 35 percent even in 1950.[53] The figure declined to about 20 percent in 1960, 11 percent in 1970, and about 8 percent in 1976.

That some of the massive buildings of public housing constructed before and during the 1960s are now viewed as eyesores is not denied; indeed, some are tragic failures. During the process, however, the government learned from its mistakes and the programs changed course. Alternatives to the construction of huge housing complexes were increasingly emphasized in the housing programs of the 1960s and 1970s: far smaller projects, public purchase of privately built housing, subsidies to builders of low-income housing, income supplements to help impoverished persons rent private housing, subsidies on mortgages to help low-income persons purchase housing, and other programs to enable low-income people to obtain decent housing through the private sector. These and earlier government housing programs, combined with the private market, have served since 1940 to reduce the percentage of Americans living in overcrowded and substandard housing by three-quarters or more.

## Job Assistance and Early Education

In the view of some, each of the programs discussed to this point lacked an essential element. However much progress took place along the nutritional, health, and housing fronts, many Americans thought that the various income and in-kind transfer programs failed to strike at the core of the poverty problem. There was only one real solution to poverty, according to this view, only one solution that could substantially end the need for programs involving massive subsidies and transfers of income. This solution, simply, was to provide people with the skills needed to obtain a self-sustaining livelihood through full-time employment. The manpower programs of government (job training and job creation) were established with this objective in mind.

Sometimes we forget, however, that full-time employment is not always feasible for large numbers of people: for the elderly, for the permanently ill or disabled, and possibly also for most single heads of families with very young children. Many millions of impoverished Americans are members of these groups. The manpower programs were relevant to comparatively few of these people. To enable these Americans to rise out of poverty, the various direct assistance and in-kind programs of government constitute the only realistic help that could have been made available. Nothing else would substitute.

Yet there remain outside these groups hundreds of thousands of other Americans with very low levels of education, many not having finished high school or perhaps even the eighth grade and many with virtually no job skills. Job-training programs might help them. In 1970, one in five males in the American labor force had not gone beyond the eighth grade.[54] Many of these people were unemployed. Others, though employed, earned only a subsistence living. Consequently, more than a million American families headed by a fully employed

43

person continued to live in poverty.

The objective of the government's job-training and job-creation programs was to speak to the situations of these people as well as the many other Americans who confronted an intensely crowded labor market in the onrush of the postwar baby boom. Here we look at what were by far the largest of the programs for adults. The Manpower Development and Training Act (MDTA), a general job-training program for unemployed adults, was established in 1962 with the purpose of training participants in skills essential to the private sector. Under the subsequent Comprehensive Employment and Training Act (CETA), which began for adults in 1973, the government became an employer of last resort by directly creating full-time public-service jobs for unemployed persons. Most jobs were intended to be temporary, designed to provide transitional employment until the participants could locate jobs in the private sector. Meanwhile, the public-service jobs would hopefully enhance the participants' skills and thus increase their job opportunities in the private sector.

How successful were these programs? The most thorough study on the results of governmental programs over the long term concerns the effects of job training and job creation under the Comprehensive Employment and Training Act. This study, the first of its kind, examined the employment careers of people for the five years subsequent to their CETA employment, covering the histories of 1,136 workers in and around the Baltimore area from 1973 through 1978. Most of the CETA participants were members of groups traditionally hard hit by

44

unemployment; 60 percent were black. The study, carried out by Johns Hopkins University, took seven years to complete.

The Johns Hopkins team discovered that the employment of CETA participants jumped significantly following participation in the CETA program and that it continued to improve over the long term.[55] Of those participants who had not been employed at all during the entire year preceding entry into CETA, 40 percent became employed immediately upon terminating the program, and 56 percent were employed within six months. Of all program participants, 48 percent found jobs immediately after leaving the program, 59 percent within one month, and 66 percent after six months. The employment rates of the CETA participants continued to climb thereafter, despite the rise in unemployment in the Baltimore area for the labor force as a whole. After five years, only 6 percent of the former CETA participants were looking for jobs.

The findings of the Baltimore study also show a significant increase in the wage levels of the CETA participants.[56] Comparing the wages of the participants employed before entering CETA with the real wages (after discounting for inflation) earned by the same participants after completing the program indicates an increase of 15 percent. Starting at 70 percent of the average wage in the Baltimore area, CETA participants had advanced to 89 percent of the average wage by 1978. The results of the only long-term analysis of a public jobs program suggest that the program was quite successful and that the program's impact did not diminish.

However, not all CETA programs brought the high level of success found by the Johns Hopkins team; indeed, some became abject failures. An extensive review of the short-term effects of more than two dozen CETA programs across the nation, undertaken on behalf of the National Academy of Sciences and published in 1978, found mixed results. Nevertheless, while calling for amendments to tighten the CETA job placement function and to place more emphasis on the severely disadvantaged, the report concluded that the overall results favored CETA and called for its reauthorization.[57]

Analyses of the federal government's job-training programs under the earlier Manpower Development and Training Act have found, even more uniformly, that these programs produced effective results. By 1965, seven of ten graduates of MDTA training programs had been placed in the type of job for which they had been trained, including 94 percent of the particpants completing on-the-job training.[58] The overall dropout rate was less than that of the nation's high schools.[59] Some estimates indicated that the taxes paid by the newly employed MDTA graduates would repay the costs of their training in five years. Nearly every study of the Manpower Training and Development Act programs published after 1965 through to the establishment of CETA found similar results. Of the assessments using cost-benefit analysis, the total benefits arising from the programs exceeded total costs in almost every case, at times surpassing an excess benefit over cost by more than 100 percent.[60]

46

The conclusion of a four-city study of job-training programs in Boston, Denver, and San Francisco-Oakland offers an indication of the impressive effects obtained by the programs:

Across all cities and programs, and despite unfavorable economic conditions, the average enrollee in an institutional training program was substantially better off in terms of employment stability and earnings because of his program participation. The lower the pre-training wage rate, the greater the wage and earnings gain was likely to be.[61]

Most studies have discovered that the results of on-the-job training programs are even superior to those of the in-house or institutional programs.[62] In short, the great majority of cost-effectiveness studies on the manpower training programs suggest that these programs benefited not only hundreds of thousands of participants but also the nation and the taxpayer.

Standing at the other end of the spectrum from the adult job-training and job-creation programs is the concept of Head Start. The Head Start program was devised to provide superior early education for lower-income children to prepare them for the school environment and subsequent employment without need for later training. On the average, Head Start has reached about 300,000 children a year, or about 20 percent of all eligible low-income children.

The foremost study on the effects of Head Start, undertaken during the 1970s, analyzed the impact of fourteen Head Start programs across the nation.[63] A majority of the children examined by the study had been randomly selected for the programs from among all low-income children in the community. Thus, most of the children who entered these Head Start programs were similar to other low-income children in the same community.

In comparing children who participated in Head Start with those who did not, the study found that children who participated before the age of 6 were about 60 percent less likely to be assigned to special education classes in grade school or high school (thereby producing a savings for their school systems); were about 45 percent less likely to be held back a grade (again producing a substantial savings to the schools); exhibited a 7-point increase in their IQ scores as an immediate result of the program, with a long-term increase on average of about half that; had more favorable perceptions of the quality of their schoolwork when in high school than did their non-Head Start cohorts; and were more likely to want to pursue higher education at a college or university. Needless to say, the parents of the Head Start children were practically unanimous in their enthusiasm for the program, a feeling that remained even among those parents who were interviewed almost a decade later.

Did the benefits exceed the costs? In reducing the number of children who otherwise would have been held back in grade or who would have required special education later and other such benefits, one study estimates that the benefits of Head Start have amounted to approximately double the costs.[64]

## *Summary*

From all the evidence concerning poverty in America and the impact of governmental programs that have attempted to redress poverty, three observations stand out. First, poverty in America cannot always be overcome by working continuously full time. To this reality, more than 5 million members of American families can testify even today. Second, vigorous economic growth in the private sector does not necessarily reduce poverty more than marginally. The years of some of the greatest sustained peacetime economic growth in many generations—the economic growth of the middle years of the post-Eisenhower era—powerfully attest to this point. Third, the government's programs to attack poverty, though at times seriously flawed, frequently were effective. They reduced poverty by more than half. They alleviated some of the grimmest conditions attendant to poverty, and they did so across the whole range of human needs pertaining to serious malnutrition, inadequate medical care, and overcrowded housing. In providing job training, they raised the economic fortunes of thousands of Americans. In providing early education to low-income children, they increased the potential of a great number of these children for success in both school and later employment.

The post-Eisenhower years were more difficult than we sometimes realize. With the spill of workers into the American labor force from 1965 through the 1970s and even beyond, the nation faced a combination of potentially explosive circumstances. Because the number of job seekers climbed rapidly, even the enormous economic growth of the post-Eisenhower years and the vastly quickened pace with which new jobs came into being would prove inadequate in providing sufficient employment. Whereas many people in the stronger economic groups could take advantage of the great prosperity of these years, some more than doubling their real incomes, those people in the weaker, less competitive economic groups, those groups that entered the era disproportionately impoverished, would be overwhelmed by the intense competition for jobs. Many of these people—the elderly, women, people with low levels of education, and the younger adults of the weakest groups—were left virtually untouched by the substantial economic growth of the day. In light of this, the economic disparity between the weaker and the stronger economic groups could only grow larger, possibly far larger, without the presence of some compensating mechanism. A most basic goal of the attack on poverty was to assure that all Americans benefited from the nation's economic expansion. The programs generated little change in the distribution of incomes in the nation during the whole of the post-Eisenhower era.[65] In line with the objective just mentioned, however, the attack on poverty did assure that the benefits brought by the nation's rapidly expanding economy would be shared by both the stronger and the weaker groups. In 1980, one in fifteen Americans faced the desperation of poverty, compared with about one in five Americans just a generation earlier. This was accomplished, almost entirely, by the government.

Was a better or cheaper avenue available to the government? "What if" questions do not, by their very nature, permit fully conclusive answers. The main alternative to the current series of individual programs is an amalgamation of the separate programs into a single, overarching structure founded upon a guaranteed income, or negative income tax. Aside from the low levels of popular support received by guaranteed-income plans during much of the post-Eisenhower period, questions have also been raised that such plans would cost more, perhaps far more, than the welfare programs have.[66] Numerous experimental trials based on the guaranteed-income concept have tended to report mixed and inconclusive results.[67] While these considerations leave uncertain exactly how well a guaranteed income would have performed, they do suggest that governmental anti-poverty action on a moderate scale would not have worked. Even the most powerful alternative to the government's programs, it appears, would have been unable to reduce poverty effectively unless accorded a level of funding from the public treasury much the same as that which the government's programs had involved.[68]

## Environmental Protection

I was there in 1961, just after finishing college, walking along the edge of Lake Erie. The memory remains vivid. Beach after beach was polluted. Signs were posted in the shallow water warning against swimming. Sledge and oil slime appeared to the naked eye, perhaps the result of passing ships. I walked farther. Garbage spewed into the lake from the great hulk of a manufacturing plant that I passed. Off in the distance, I could see dozens of other industrial plants lining the shore. Everywhere around me, it seemed, the walleye pike of this famous lake floated atop the water. The signs were unmistakable: The lake was dying. I did not stop to consider whether the process was reversible. To me, at that time, the death of our lakes was simply the inevitable price of industrialization.

Now, twenty-five years later, it seems unsurprising that in the affluent and prosperous post-Eisenhower years a public outcry would follow the degradation of our environment, and that following the outcry the federal government would intervene. This stands as the second major undertaking of the nation's government during the post-Eisenhower years. When Rachael Carson's *Silent Spring* was published in 1962, it ignited the environmental movement. Between 1963 and 1980, Congress adopted legislation intended to bring air and water pollution under control, foster coastal zone and other land-use planning, control strip mining, protect Alaskan lands, and regulate toxic wastes.

As in the case of the poverty programs, the environmental programs have come under heavy fire. Repeatedly, attempts are made to reduce their funding and to confine their power. Like the poverty programs, too, the environmental programs enacted by the government have brought about substantial progress in some areas and at the least have prevented great backsliding in others. Still a third characteristic shared by the environmental and poverty programs is that success could not have been achieved without massive governmental intervention. The presence of an enormous governmental effort was—and is still—called for.

By the late 1950s and the early 1960s, environmental pollution had become an expensive problem in the United States. In a whole string of urban areas across the nation, more than one-third of the year was marked by hazardous or unhealthful air pollution. Estimates for 1968 indicated that without environmental controls air pollution in the nation would have cost more than $16 billion in damage.[69] About $5 billion of that cost would stem from air-pollution damage to residential and commercial property, requiring large expenditures for resurfacing and rebuilding. But the cost to the nation in the deterioration of buildings and housing was only one element. Substantial costs would also arise from the harmful effects of air pollution on health. Reflected in such items as increased medical bills and days lost at work, these costs would have amounted to more than $6 billion in 1968.

Throughout the late 1950s and the 1960s the federal government had prodded state governments and private industry to deal with the growing problems of pollution voluntarily. The Water Pollution Control Act of 1956 and the Clean Air Act of 1963 called upon the states and other interested parties to convene conferences to study the increased incidences of pollution and to develop standards and plans by which to control pollution. The Clean Air Act of 1963 enabled the federal government to provide financial grants to states and localities. Following the act, spending to combat air pollution increased by more than 50 percent in the first two years and sixfold by the end of the decade. By 1965–66, 58 percent of the urban public was served by local air-pollution-control programs. The spending in these localities for the programs had reached about 40 percent of what was considered adequate for effective action.[70]

But far less action had taken place at the state and the regional levels and even in some urban localities. Indeed, by 1970, no state had yet fully implemented an air-quality plan.[71] Moreover, the standards to control water pollution were inadequate in almost every state, a result of the fear that stronger measures would discourage new industry. As a consequence, the standards set in states with the worst water quality became the *norm* for states across the nation.[72]

The period 1956–70 demonstrated that while some progress could be achieved through voluntary action and federal grants, stronger federal measures were needed to move the states as well as the more resistant urban areas into action. Thus, the Congress amended the Clean Air Act in 1970 and the Water Pollution Control Act in 1972. Even many leading conservative economists had come to agree that firm governmental action was needed, although they disagreed with the particular form that such action was to take (Appendix B).

Considering the policy of the past, the actions that the Congress took involved radical policy changes. The 1970 amendments to the Clean Air Act gave a national agent, the Environmental Protection Agency, the authority to set national air-quality performance standards. Should states not draw up plans within a reasonable period to meet the standards, the amendments gave the EPA the power to do so. The Water Pollution Control Act amendments of 1972 likewise established goals for water quality that were to be met nationwide. Private businesses and industry were directed to adopt the "best practicable" technology for waste treatment by 1977 and the "best available" technology by 1983. A nationwide discharge-permit system was authorized, and the EPA was given the power to administer and enforce the system. A discharge permit specified the amount of pollutant that could be emitted from each installation. Finally, to help state and local governments meet sewage disposal needs, federal funding would contribute three-quarters of the financing for constructing local waste treatment plants, with a projected cost of $6 billion annually.

## The Results of Environmental Programs: Air Quality

Initiated by the rapid economic growth of the post-Eisenhower era, substantial expansion in economic activity occurred during the years after 1960 that might be expected to aggravate air and water pollution. In just the years from 1965 to 1980, the nation's economy grew by more than 40 percent after adjusting for inflation. Industrial production rose at a fast pace, too, climbing by more than 50 percent. The use of all forms of energy increased dramatically. Even the consumption of coal rose. Contrary to the impression that cleaner-burning oil replaced

55

coal and that the use of coal thereby declined, the nation's consumption of coal actually increased by more than 15 percent from 1965 through 1979.

How did the nation's environment fare in the midst of these developments? In the case of air pollution, spending under governmental programs increased sharply between 1963 and 1970, and of course the programs were able to aim at levels of pollution that were the easiest and least costly to remove. Business and industry are at one in pointing out that the costs of reducing pollution increase dramatically as one moves toward removing its last vestiges. The figures available for 1960–70 reveal that levels of particulate matter (soot and dust) in the air declined hardly at all from 1960 to 1965 and then steadily fell by almost 20 percent from 1965 to 1970.[73] Figures for 1963–70 are also available on the amounts of sulfur dioxide (derived largely from the burning of coal and oil) in the air. These figures show little improvement from 1963 to 1966 and then a steady decline in airborne sulfur dioxide of almost 60 percent from 1966 to 1970.[74]

General data are available for other components of air pollution only in the 1970s. After 1970, both sulfur dioxide and suspended particulate matter continued the rapid declines that had begun earlier.[75] By 1979, the level of sulfur dioxide in the air had declined by about an additional 40 percent from its level in 1970; concentrations of suspended particulate matter in the air in 1979 had declined by an additional 17 percent from their 1970 level. For carbon monoxide (from automobile exhaust) the decline was almost 40 percent in the 1970s. On the other hand, there was less success with ozone (an element of smog) pollution levels, which remained constant during the decade, and with nitrogen dioxide (another element of smog), which actually increased by 12 percent over the decade. The nationwide results for annual average concentrations thus show considerable progress in three of the five standard pollutants, constancy in one, and retrogression in one (the one, perhaps not coincidentally, that is the most difficult pollutant to measure properly).[76]

Peak air pollution is also tracked in the nation's urban areas. In 1973–74 air-pollution levels in ten major urban areas were classified as unhealthful, very unhealthful, or hazardous during at least one-third of the days.[77] Air pollution declined in each and every one of these urban areas. By 1979–80, the number of days of excessive peak air pollution had been reduced by 35 percent on average in these urban areas.[78] In fact, in all twenty-three urban areas measured around the nation the number of hazardous and very unhealthful days of air pollution declined by about 30 percent from 1974 through 1979, and the days of unhealthful air pollution declined by 12 percent over those years.[79]

Progress is also reflected in the improving emission records of new automobiles. The 1970 amendments to the Clean Air Act called for significant reductions in emissions by new automobiles on pain of stiff fines for offending vehicles. By 1978, the emission of hydrocarbons by new automobiles had declined by more than two-thirds and that of carbon monoxide and nitrogen oxides had declined by half and one-third, respectively.[80]

## The Results of Environmental Programs: Water Quality

The situation concerning water pollution is more uncertain. Water-pollution legislation, including the 1972 controls, regulates only "point sources" of pollution, that is, pollution that is discharged by way of a discrete (usually stationary) pipe or outfall or ditch. The regulations do not cover the sources of more than half the pollution entering the water: runoff into the water of fertilizers, oils, soaps, and other chemicals from urban and suburban private residences, yards, streets, parking lots, and the nation's farms. Runoff of pollution from such sources is difficult to control and cannot be measured as easily as, say, air pollution from private automobiles.

But even the regulation of less than half the input of pollution indicates that after 1974 further degradation of the nation's waters was curbed; no overall decline in water quality was found following 1974.[81] In fact, where meaningful changes in water-pollution violation rates did occur, water pollution generally diminished. In those urban areas monitored by the Council on Environmental Quality in which the rates of water pollution violation noticeably changed, violations measured by the presence of fecal coliform bacteria (generated mostly by improperly treated human and animal feces) fell in 22 of 26 cases; violations measured by levels of dissolved oxygen (often generated by untreated sewage) fell in 11 of 14 cases; violations measured by levels of biochemical oxygen demand (generated by organic waste) fell in 6 of 9 cases; and violations measured by total phosphorus in the water fell in 13 of 17 cases.[82] Additional progress in the improvement of nation's water quality was suggested by the reduction of industrial violations toward the end of the 1970s. Such violations declined more than 20 percent from 1978 to 1980.

Still another indication of improvement is the situation in the Great Lakes, the lakes whose death once seemed imminent. In these lakes resides 20 percent of the world's fresh water supply. To the growing environmental movement in the 1960s, Lake Erie and Lake Ontario were among the chief exhibits of the deterioration of the nation's waters. But testimony about Lake Ontario at the Conference of the International Association for the Great Lakes Research in 1981 reveals that levels of major contaminants in the lake declined significantly during the latter 1970s.[83] Today Lake Erie is alive with fish. The pike, whose lifeless remains once crowded the shores, are now flourishing within its waters.

According to the National Wildlife Federation, an organization with stringent standards, about fifty major bodies of water showed considerable improvement over the decade of the 1970s. In addition, the Wildlife Federation estimated that by 1980 "approximately 3600 of the nation's 4000 largest industrial polluters, or about 90 percent, [were] meeting their clean-up deadlines."[84]

## Benefits and Costs of Environmental Programs

The nation thus experienced an absolute reversal in air pollution trends during the 1960s and 1970s; it also avoided further deterioration of its waters, the area in which governmental regulation was most confined. As with progress against poverty, these accomplishments are well worth attention, though certainly they remain some distance from perfection.

Although it is difficult to measure the total costs and benefits of pollution control with great precision, an attempt to do so was made by the Council on Environmental Quality in a report that consolidated the findings of a series of independent 1978 studies that had separately attempted to calculate costs and benefits. The report found that in 1978 the benefits of air-pollution controls with respect to health and other concerns could be reasonably estimated at about $21.4 billion. The costs borne by government to administer air-pollution controls, and by the private sector to purchase and install pollution controls, totaled about $16.6 billion.[85] A similar estimate for the 1970s for the water-pollution control programs is not available.[86]

This is not to argue that the policies cannot be improved. A mounting body of evidence indicates that some of the pollutants currently regulated cause more harm to health in the long term than do others, suggesting that the benefits of pollution control might be increased without raising the cost by elevating standards on the more harmful pollutants while relaxing standards somewhat on less harmful pollutants. At present, too, the government's policy puts enormous efforts into waste-treatment plants, which do little to affect non-point sources of water pollution, the cause of at least half of all water pollution. Perhaps here, too, the benefits of control could be increased without raising the overall cost if less emphasis was placed on waste treatment and more attention was given to nonpoint sources of pollution. These and other such examples point to the need to refine, and in some cases redirect, the current approach. They do not suggest scrapping the present approach for another,[87] or reducing the regulatory requirements now in effect without achieving a balance by upgrading standards even further in the areas that would likely profit most.[88]

## Waste in Government

Of all the biting criticisms to emerge from the post-Eisenhower era, the idea that waste ran rampant in the domestic programs of the government stands as perhaps the most universally believed. The view that the government wasted excessive amounts of money created unsettled attitudes toward the government's programs almost across the board. One story after another appeared. One day it was about widespread fraud in the Medicaid program, the next day about a welfare cheater found living at the Plaza. Such a consensus prevailed regarding waste that no disagreement was to be found among the presidential candidates. All the presidential candidates in the 1976 and 1980 campaigns agreed that government wasted much money and manpower. All agreed that substantial cuts in the budget could be achieved by eliminating waste in government. Candidates spoke of the billions of dollars and millions of man hours that could be saved. "Cut waste," "cut abuse," "cut extravagance," and "cut fraud" were everywhere the bywords as the candidates talked about how to cut federal spending and balance the budget.

Waste, abuse, extravagance, and fraud—exactly how serious were these four components of government inefficiency? "I call [them] the four horsemen of the budget apocalypse. Actually, they are tired old nags that have been trotted out by every presidential challenger. No more than $4 billion could be saved that way,"[89] according to one respected economist, Walter Heller, professor of economics at the University of Minnesota and former chairman of the Council of Economic Advisers.

But Heller had advised the Democrats, the party that had devised and implemented most of the domestic programs. The Republicans, on the other hand, did not have to defend the programs. In 1980, moreover, the Republicans were out of power. They had every incentive to uncover and report all the waste in the domestic programs they could find. With this in mind, a member of the Republican Study Committee of the House of Representatives, in preparation for the 1980 campaign, requested the committee's staff to compile and publish a detailed report on the topic of waste, fraud, mismanagement, and abuse in government.[90] The special report that followed encompassed the entire range of governmental programs. Based primarily on the investigations of the General Accounting Office, the report also included criticisms of programs made by the inspectors general of various of the departments. The report boldly announced that there existed in documented form more than $34 billion in waste, fraud, abuse, and mismanagement, a figure that was bandied about quite freely during the 1980 campaign. Because the Republicans proposed to increase defense spending, it was only natural to presume that most of the waste came from domestic programs.

Few noticed that about half the waste identified in the report came, amazingly, not from the domestic areas at all but from the foreign and defense areas.[91] All the domestic programs taken together were responsible for only about half. Also, the span of time the report covered was not a year but eighteen months. When adjusted for these considerations, the report had actually divulged a yearly total of $11.8 billion in waste in the functioning of the domestic programs—not a spindly sum, to be sure, but nevertheless a great distance from the created impression of more than $30 billion of waste annually in the domestic realm. Since overall domestic spending totaled approximately $370 billion in 1979, the inefficiencies in the domestic realm attributed by the special report to the four horsemen of the budget apocalypse amounted to about 3 percent.

But there was to be another try at the matter in the drive to reduce federal spending. Shortly after taking the oath of office, President Reagan proposed reductions of about $40 billion in the projected spending of the domestic programs. To help achieve such economies, the president established his own committee to identify and investigate waste in all areas of the government's programs. Calling it the Council on Integrity and Efficiency, he named Edwin Harper, deputy director of the Office of Management and Budget, to head the council. Harper's boss was none other than David Stockman, a renowned budget cutter. The council issued its first report after six months of work. It had by then identified waste, abuse, and fraud totaling around $4 billion, just about what Walter Heller had predicted a year earlier, some months before the 1980 election.[92] Moreover, only $1.1 billion of this amount came from the domestic programs; the remaining $2.9 billion came from within the defense establishment. There is an important implication here. It means that 97 percent of the $40 billion proposed by the president to be cut from domestic programs would have to come from areas other than those identified by the council as wasteful. Looking to the future, Harper estimated that the council would be able to find waste in the domestic and defense programs totaling around $7.5 billion a year in the 1981–83 period, or about 2 percent of the total federal budget. Considering that the defense area comprises half the waste, the loss resulting from fraud, abuse, and waste in the domestic programs represents less than one cent on the dollar of domestic spending.

In any human enterprise, waste is bound to occur. The questions are how much and compared to what alternative. I have presented some estimates about how much from sources with every incentive to enlarge the figure. In the realm of comparisons, the private business sector offers a reasonable yardstick. If one thinks seriously about comparisons, some extraordinary efficiencies of government begin immediately to leap to mind.

Consider the matter of salaries. In 1978 the average salary of the top five hundred federal officials was around $65,000 per year. The top five hundred officials in private business averaged more than four times this annual salary, or $275,000 per year. Over $100 million in difference existed yearly between government and private industry in the salaries of these sets of five hundred individuals alone. Pay of a half million dollars or more a year was not uncommon. The best-paid banker in 1980 received practically as much as did all the members of the president's cabinet taken together. Indeed, literally hundreds of thousands of people in industry, medicine, law, banking, and accounting and brokerage firms received sums far exceeding those received by any member of the Senate or the House of Representatives, any member of their staffs, any member of the president's cabinet, the head of any federal agency, or indeed any federal bureaucrat. This continues today.

It didn't take long for members of the Reagan administration to appreciate that leaders of government work long hours for comparatively little money. Soon after taking office as the new administration's secretary of the treasury, Donald Regan was asked what his greatest surprise had been since coming to the Capital:

[It's] the long hours that people work for so little money. . . . Our people are in here by 7:30 in the morning, certainly by 8. When I left last night at twenty of eight, there were still people around here working, which is a thirteen-hour day. Plus homework and weekends, you've got people working 70, 80, and 90 hours a week for what I know are salaries that are less than a third they could command in the private sector.[93]

Very long hours are typical in Congress as well, among both members and staffers.[94] After his defeat in the 1980 election and return to the private sector, former Senator Gaylord Nelson quipped to a Wisconsin audience: "Now I work half the hours for twice the pay." With respect to the top salaries of governmental officials, an efficiency exists in the public sector completely untouched by the private sector.

Efficiencies also abound elsewhere in government. Compare the offices built over the last two decades of almost any government with the offices built over those same years by private sector businesses or industries that operate on a comparable yearly budget. The head offices of government, such as city or county halls, almost all look cheap by comparison, with standard vinyl flooring, bare block walls, curtainless windows, few if any decorations, and institutional metal furniture. Because cost efficiency has been a top priority in the building and furnishing of most government buildings over the last twenty years, hardly any government offices built during that period come close to matching the expensive, glittering, often opulent showcases that are everywhere evident in the private world of business and industry.

Nor should one ignore the fraud and abuse that occurs in private businesses. In the middle of the 1970s the United States Chamber of Commerce calculated that fraud, embezzlement, and other forms of white-collar crime totaled as much as $40 billion a year in private business and industry, costs that (like the top salaries and the showcase headquarters) are largely passed on to the consumer.[95] Forty billion dollars represented at the time about 4 percent of all business revenue annually; this is somewhat greater than the percentage alleged to occur in *all* forms of loss (waste as well as fraud and abuse) in the federal government's domestic programs,[96] as reported by either the staff of the Republican Study Committee or President Reagan's council.

Productivity assessments afford still another measure of the success of government domestic programs compared with that of private business. Measures of government productivity (total output per employee) are available over the period from 1967 to 1978. Appraisals of productivity in the federal government indicate that total output per employee improved by 17 percent from 1967 to 1978, including a productivity improvement of 32 percent in the area of social programs (social services and benefits). During those same years, the productivity of employees in all private nonfarm businesses improved by 16 percent.[97]

No one knows for certain how much waste and abuse exists anywhere, neither in the world of government nor in the private sector. By their very nature, these remain matters that human beings do their very best to hide. Estimates thus become all that is possible. Waste exists in the domestic programs of government, and the efforts to reduce it are appropriate. Some programs may be much more wasteful than others. But if the various overall estimates cited here are even close to approximating reality, waste is far below what it is generally alleged to be. The array of evidence offered, taken in its entirety, suggests that the domestic programs of government have been run more efficiently than the defense programs and as efficiently as the affairs of private industry. The overall estimates, from quarters that had every incentive to enlarge them, reveal that waste in domestic programs most typically existed more at the margins than at the core. With respect to the domestic sphere, the estimates indicate that some budget economies were possible, but that even the elimination of all waste would have been unable to bring vast budget savings.

## Conclusion

Citizens have every right to ask that governmental programs achieve positive ends, that they do so to a degree the private economy could not accomplish, and that the level of waste and abuse be limited. In general, the domestic programs of government that we have surveyed after 1960 appear to have fared reasonably well in these respects.

The introduction and enlargement after 1960 of the many governmental programs to reduce poverty and environmental pollution were associated with solid progress over a broad spectrum of national concerns. During the twenty years of the post-Eisenhower era, the government's programs led to a diminishing of poverty among Americans by more than half. They significantly reduced flagrant malnutrition, lessened inequality in access to medical services, and were associated with dramatic declines in infant mortality rates among the poor and the minorities. They helped relieve over-crowded and substandard housing. They also improved the education of impoverished children and gave employable skills to thousands of otherwise unemployed adults. In the wake of the environmental programs, pollution levels in the nation's air were generally reversed, and pollution of the nation's waters was checked. A single generation of Americans realized these accomplishments, enough perhaps for any generation to leave as its legacy. Notwithstanding the crescendo of criticism that ushered out the decade of the 1970s, the post-Eisenhower era was in fact an age of distinguished public achievement.

Nor could such advances have been brought about without large-scale governmental programs. And this is the very crux of the matter. A key lesson of the post-Eisenhower era is that the government's domestic programs grew to be large because no other plan of action could have worked. This is as true of the fight to reduce poverty as it is of the struggle against environmental pollution.

Yet, could the nation afford the programs' costs? True, many positive results were realized. True, the private sector could not have matched those results, nor was any other avenue of governmental intervention obviously superior. And it is also true that waste in the programs was probably far less than is often assumed.

Ultimately, however, the question arises about the cost, amounting to billions of dollars in governmental spending and regulation every year. Were not these and the other programs of government so expensive as to place financial and regulatory burdens on Americans, eventually causing the nation's economy to suffer? If true, the programs could legitimately be thought to share responsibility for the economic difficulties that faced the nation, and in this would unwittingly have sown the seeds of their own demise. Without a prosperous economy, the political support that stood behind efforts to overcome poverty and pollution, both still unfinished tasks, was bound to erode.

# 3

## The Political Legacy of the 1960s and 1970s: Runaway Government and a Stagnant Economy?

"THAT GOVERNMENT IS BEST which governs least," said Thomas Jefferson, whose familiar phrase still carries great currency in American political thinking. It remains a standard people use to evaluate and, in the case of the post-Eisenhower years, to criticize the government's performance. The notion that the government had grown excessively, and that it attempted to do too much,[1] stood at the forefront of debate at the end of the post-Eisenhower years. Many championed the theme that the government's unbridled growth was responsible for the downward trend in the nation's economy.[2] Only by stopping that growth and removing the overwhelming burden of government from the backs of the American taxpayer and the American businessman, it was said, could the nation's economy regain strength and once again produce unmatched economic success. With generations of the Jeffersonian ideal behind us, the nation was ready to believe that its government had become too large.

Exactly how much such ideas influenced votes is hard to say. But increasing numbers of Americans felt that government had gotten out of control. Between 1965 and 1980 alone, spending on social programs had risen from 5 to 11 percent of the GNP. Relentlessly, the government swelled in size and power, it seemed, apparently knowing no bounds. Unbounded, too, were the numbers of ways in which the government's rampant growth was considered harmful to the economy. Government had been "taxing away the American way of life," President Reagan told us a few months after he had entered office.[3] Among the alleged effects of big government were the slowing of economic growth and profits, the decline in business investment and worker productivity, and the increase in inflation. All these keys to our nation's poor economic performance could be reversed, the critics argued, if we could find the will to contain the reach of government. All would have been changed for the better, it was claimed, if only that determination to limit growth had been found earlier.[4] The economy's vitality, and our prosperity, lay victim to big government.

Although frequently heard at the close of the 1970s, these contentions about the government's expansion and its consequences for the nation's economy were, and remain today, founded largely upon a set of myths. The myths seemed so patently true on the surface that few people looked further. But they stand nonetheless as myths. No unbridled growth of the nation's government took place from 1960 to 1980; instead, in most respects, the government grew very slightly in the 1960s and 1970s in relation to the size of the nation's economy. This is the case whether one considers taxation, deficit spending, the size of the bureaucracy, or the amount of regulation; in fact, with but a few exceptions, the government actually grew at a faster pace during the Eisenhower era than it did in the 1960s and 1970s. What, then, of the supposed dire consequences for our economy brought about by the increasingly heavier burden of government? Enter yet another myth, for the economy of the 1970s, let alone that of the 1960s, generally expanded at a brisk pace, certainly when compared with the decade of the 1950s. This conclusion applies to almost all economic concerns, including the growth rates of production, real income, investment, employment, and, in some important respects, even productivity. Thus, the familiar assertions are not only wrong; often they are backward. The opposite images are most often more accurate. What is claimed as having occurred (excessive growth in the size of government) in most respects did not take place. What is claimed as not having occurred (reasonably rapid rates of economic growth) largely did take place. The series of upside-down images detailed in this chapter, like those about the government's programs developed in the preceding pages, suggest that to understand our recent history will require a decisive change in many of the attitudes we came to hold about our government and economy as the nation emerged from the post-Eisenhower years.

The following evidence may seem baffling, even outrageous. One after another, the conclusions of the chapter run contrary to the new consensus of thought that swept aside all in its path as the post-Eisenhower years ended. My hope is that readers will find the conclusions ever more believable as we proceed. The record of evidence of the years from 1960 to 1980 in this chapter disputes almost every tenet of the now-dominant ideology's critique of both unbridled governmental expansion and an economy grown increasingly stagnant.

Nor does the evidence depend in any sense upon odd or remote publications. Neither is it necessary to call upon the word of "experts," whom the reader may or may not know or respect. The evidence behind almost all the conclusions, including those about taxation, the federal deficit, the bureaucracy, and the state of the economy, comes directly from a single, highly reputable source, *The Statistical Abstract of the United States,* compiled by the Bureau of the Census. It is a widely available official source, and the facts are there for anyone to see. I will carefully note any exceptions by citing other sources when this becomes appropriate. Because the *Abstract* contains little information on the costs of regulation, in this area alone will there be a need to go outside it as a general rule. Here, to be on as undisputed ground as possible, I draw my evidence entirely from the same figures the critics themselves use.

The belief that government greatly extended its grip on the American economy and society deserves careful investigation, especially with respect to two unique features about governmental power. One feature concerns what we might call the government's "extractive capacity": This is government's capacity to command economic resources that under free-market conditions might go elsewhere (presumably, free-market theorists would claim, to more efficient and productive uses). The principal extractive powers of the government are the powers to tax income, profits, capital, and property and to enter into debt. The second salient power of the government is its regulatory power, that is, its ability to regulate the behavior of businesses and private individuals.

When one considers the meaning behind the now-common assertions concerning the need to get government off the backs of the American people, it is primarily the extractive and regulatory powers of government —and the supposed great extension of government power in those areas—to which such statements refer. Certainly the Reagan administration has given great emphasis to these areas—to reducing general revenue taxes (particularly personal and corporate income taxes) and to easing regulations on the private business sector. It is thus proper to ask to what extent government in the United States had extended its power in these important areas during the post-Eisenhower decades leading to 1980 and to what extent its growth in these areas deflected the nation's economic performance.

## The Growth of Government: Taxation

I have not taken count, but I would wager that high taxation provides the single topic upon which letters to newspapers are most vitriolic and for which one finds the fewest responses on the other side. The words contained in the letters convey an enormously intense feeling, amounting almost to rage: "fed up," "sick and tired," "oppressed," and "sucked dry" are just some of the terms used. So, too, do descriptions of the alleged culprits tell a tale of rising fury, the references to all the "bleeding hearts" who think "the taxpayer's wallet is up for grabs." We have, each one of us, read such letters, and the deep anger they express is extremely moving.

What happened, then, to taxes during the post-Eisenhower years? Forms of taxation that we traditionally consider part of general revenue available to the government include personal and corporate income taxes, property taxes, and sales and customs taxes. Not until the last decade did the revenues of the insurance trust funds (the biggest of which is social security) become officially attached to the federal budget. For the preceding four decades, the budget did not embrace the trust funds. These funds were kept separate largely because the monies that entered the trusts could, ultimately, be spent only for the general purposes of the trusts, thereby granting the government limited discretion over use of the funds. They were not, and still are not, part of general revenue. In the following argument about the size of the tax bite into our dollar, I first consider the entire scope of the budget with respect to general revenue. These are precisely the taxes that were most highly targeted as affecting the incentive of Americans to produce and invest more, and reducing them stood as the unflagging priority of the Reagan administration from the moment it took office. The discussion then moves on to consider the trust funds, and to draw conclusions about the total weight of the tax burden.

For purposes of brevity, emphasis is placed on the following sources of the government's general revenue: personal income taxes, taxes on corporate profits, and taxes on property. Sales and customs taxes or any other general revenue taxes would not change the conclusions. Together, the three sources covered here netted the federal, state, and local governments about 75 percent of all general revenues available to government over the post-Eisenhower years.[5]

Some surprising conclusions emerge if one casts presumption aside and actually looks at the size of taxes on corporate profits, individual income, and property. Corporate taxes (federal and state) as a percentage of profits began the 1960s at 47 cents per dollar of profit. (On $48.5 billion of profits in 1960, corporations paid $22.7 billion in taxes.)[6] This corporate tax in 1960 amounted to an increase of 3 cents per dollar of profit over that of five years earlier in 1955, then at 44 cents per dollar; it amounted to an increase of 5 cents per dollar of profit from 1950, when it stood at 42 cents per dollar. In contrast to an increase in corporate profits taxes of 5 percent from 1950 to 1960, the years after 1960 witnessed exactly the reverse. Starting out at 47 percent of profits in 1960, tax changes of various kinds in the 1960s and 1970s lowered corporate taxes to an average of 41 percent of profits during the 1970s and, indeed, to 39 percent of profits by the end of the post-Eisenhower years in 1979. (On $236.6 billion in profits in 1979, corporations paid $92.5 billion in taxes.) Few noticed what had amounted to a reduction in the corporate tax rate following the Eisenhower years, to a rate *lower* than it had been thirty years earlier in 1950. Far more visible was the view of William C. Freund, chief economist of the New York Stock Exchange. Contending that government's increased taxation of business was undermining the health of the economy and the ability to invest, he argued that the top focus of action to set things right in the 1980s "should be to reduce the corporate tax load."[7] That taxation as a percentage of business profits had declined since the 1950s, rather than increased, seemed unworthy of mention.

Had the average corporate tax rate grown excessively and become a burden, or had this been so for the tax rate on the last dollar of profits (known as the marginal tax rate), presumably the incentive to invest in American business would have diminished. At least that is the supply-side argument. But not even the marginal tax rate on corporation profits seems to have changed for the worse.[8] Nor, as I show later in this chapter, did rates of business investment (in terms of either gross or net investment) suffer at all during the 1970s. By whatever measure, the rate of increase in business investment in America remained as high in the 1970–80 and 1960–70 periods as it had been in the decade preceding the post-Eisenhower years, the years from 1950 to 1960.

The government's taxation of personal income, on the other hand, did rise somewhat during the post-Eisenhower years, although the rise was not anything like the monumental amount described by absolute figures. Consider the absolute figures. Americans paid $43 billion in income taxes in 1960; less than twenty years later, in what appeared to be an extraordinary increase, the $200 billion mark had been passed. No wonder Americans came to believe that the tax burden had grown excessively.

However, personal incomes had also experienced a substantial rise over those years. As a percentage of Americans' personal income, the increase in the income tax looks quite different. Income taxes (federal and state combined) amounted to 10.8 percent of Americans' personal income in 1960 and rose to 12.9 percent at the conclusion of the 1970s. The increase thus averaged 2.1 cents on a dollar of income, a moderate increase, certainly when compared with the rate of increase of Eisenhower years. During the 1950s, personal income taxes had risen from 7.2 percent of personal income in 1950 to an average of 10.8 percent at the conclusion of the Eisenhower presidency in 1960.[9] This is to say that personal income taxes rose by 3.6 points in the decade of the 1950s alone, compared with an increase of 2.1 points during the post-Eisenhower years, a period twice as long.

Approximately half the increase in personal income taxes in the 1960s and 1970s was due to state income tax increases. This is to say that, as a percentage of income, federal income taxes grew on average by only about 1 cent per dollar of income throughout the entire twenty years of the post-Eisenhower period. Readers may find this inconceivable. It becomes more plausible with concrete examples of individual family situations.[10] Consider an average middle-income family of four at the beginning of the period, in 1960, whose head earned an income of $10,000, and a middle-income family in 1979, whose head earned $25,000, or slightly more after inflation than the earnings in 1960. In 1960 such a family paid $1,372 in federal income taxes, whereas on an income of $25,000 in 1979, the family owed the federal government $3,490 in income taxes, or an absolute amount well beyond twice the income tax paid in 1960. Although the increase in absolute amount is substantial, the family actually paid approximately the same percentage of its income in 1979 as it had in 1960: The family paid 14 percent of its income in taxes to the federal government in 1979 ($3,490 of $25,000), about the same as the 13.7 percent ($1,372 of $10,000) paid in 1960. Thus, for this typical middle-income family, the federal personal income tax remained at about the same percentage of income in 1979 as it had been in 1960.

The same is true for families of lower incomes. A four-person family with a taxable income of $5,000 in 1960 would have paid, on average, 8.4 percent ($420 of $5,000) of that income in federal income taxes; the same family earning $15,000 in 1979 would have paid an average of 8.3 percent ($1,238 of $15,000) of its income in tax. The family could thus actually increase its real income (after subtracting for inflation) by about 25 percent from 1960 through 1979 and would be obliged to pay no larger a percentage of its income to the federal government.

Thinking about taxes in terms of the absolute amount rather than as a percentage of income makes it appear as if income taxes have skyrocketed. Thinking in percentages of income permits one to look at the matter from another perspective. Federal income tax rates were adjusted at several points during the post-Eisenhower years. The various tax adjustments meant that for most Americans, as in the cases we have just reviewed, people in the same income class (that is, the same real income in 1979 as in 1960 after accounting for inflation) normally paid about the same percentage of their income in 1979 as they had in 1960. That the percentage of income paid in federal income tax grew very little over the whole of the post-Eisenhower years is obscured by absolute figures. For the large majority of Americans, this same conclusion applies even to the federal income tax paid on the last dollar of personal income earned or received, known as the effective marginal rate of tax.[11]

If neither corporate nor personal income taxes rose substantially during the period after 1960, possibly the situation was different for the third major tax, property taxes.[12] Given the passage of California's Proposition 13 in early 1978 to reduce property taxes, and the subsequent adoption of similar propositions in many other states across the nation, one would surmise that government taxes on property not only had increased but had risen faster than the people's ability to pay. Once again, however, the facts tell another story. California is a prime example. In the state that produced the spectacular landslide in 1978 for the pathbreaking Proposition 13, revenues from property taxes during the last full year before the revolt, 1977, amounted to 5.8 percent of personal income in the state. How much of a property-tax increase had taken place since 1970? Actually, this represented a slight *decline* from 1970 when revenues from property taxes in California amounted to 5.9 percent of personal income in the state.

Many states followed California's lead and lowered their property taxes. As in California, property taxes across the nation, in proportion to personal income, had remained relatively constant as a general rule. Property taxes averaged 4.1 percent of the nation's personal income in 1977, a slight decline from 1970 (when it was 4.3 percent) and exactly the same as the percentage at the beginning of the post-Eisenhower years in 1960 (4.1 percent). Were a property tax revolt to be at all in order, once again it might better have come at the end of the 1950s. For during those ten years property taxes as a whole did climb from 3.3 percent of personal income in 1950 to 4.1 percent of personal income in 1960.

Since dramatic increases in taxes on personal income, property, and corporate profits did not take place on average during the years from 1960 to 1980, perhaps some other evidence led to the common belief that the total of such taxes, or indeed other taxes, had become generally excessive. An obvious possibility is the one of international comparison: the possibility that the tax bite in the United States was excessive in comparison with those of the other industrialized nations with which we were competing, or that taxes were declining in these other nations, whereas they were not in the United States.

Neither possibility turns out to be the case. West

Germany serves as an example for comparison. Currently, in the midst of a flagging international economy, the West German economy is sluggish. But during the post-Eisenhower decades the West German economy was commonly perceived to be both one of the strongest and most stable economies in the world. To facilitate international comparisons, the Organization of European Cooperation and Development (OECD) issues figures dealing with taxation in the industrialized nations. The OECD reported comparative figures for the decade of the 1970s. Its figures cover all taxes from all sources in each nation, including each nation's trust funds.[13] The OECD figures show that at the end of the period in 1979, government taxation in West Germany stood considerably higher than that in the United States. Taxation amounted to 37.3 percent of the GDP (gross domestic product) in West Germany in 1979 as compared with a total tax bite in the United States of 31.3 percent of GDP, or six points lower. Moreover, taxes in West Germany had increased from 32.8 percent in 1970 to 37.3 percent in 1979, whereas American taxes had risen more marginally, from 30.1 percent in 1970 to 31.3 percent in 1979. With the sole exception of the United Kingdom, taxes rose more from 1970 through 1979 in every other major industrialized nation examined by the OECD: Japan, 5 percent more of GDP; France, 6 percent; Italy, 2 percent; West Germany, 4 percent. Even in Switzerland, that nation renowned for its frugality, governmental taxation climbed by 7 percent during the 1970s, once more decidedly faster than the 1.2 percent of the United States.

Aside from the comparative perspective, the OECD figures reveal something else about the total level of American taxation. They indicate that American taxes (again, the figures encompass all taxes from all sources, including the trust funds) had actually increased very little from 1970 through 1979. During this last half of the post-Eisenhower period, the growth in the overall level of tax revenues as a proportion of GDP had come practically to a halt. In fact, if one employs the standard American measure of the total economy, the gross national product, total governmental receipts rose by only a minuscule 0.3 percent of GNP (from 31.4 percent to 31.7 percent) in the last eleven years (1969–80) of the post-Eisenhower era.[14] To the degree that government revenue did rise over the 1960–80 period, then, it occurred mainly from 1960 to 1969, and even then was largely the result of one tax: the insurance trusts, particularly social security. This tax climbed from 2.9 percent of GNP in 1960 to 5.9 percent in 1979, with the majority of the increase coming before 1970.[15]

*The post-Eisenhower years did not witness runaway growth in taxation by a government unable to contain itself.* Quite the reverse. American taxes had risen prior to 1960, during the Eisenhower years. But by the middle of the post-Eisenhower years the increase in total taxation as a percentage of the economy had markedly slackened, coming almost to a stop. Moreover, not one of the general revenue taxes claimed to influence economic motivation—the incentive to earn or to produce more—had increased substantially from the beginning to the end of the post-Eisenhower years. Personal income taxes grew slightly, and corporate taxes as a percentage of profits and property taxes as a percentage of personal income either remained relatively constant or declined. The alleged increases in these taxes nevertheless became subject to the harshest of criticism from both political and economic quarters. A single tax, and that tax alone, climbed appreciably over the post-Eisenhower years. This was the tax tied to the insurance trusts. And even this tax would not raise the total level of taxation more than marginally after 1969. The increase in social spending from 1969 to 1980 was funded not by an increase in taxation but mainly by tempering other spending, for example, spending on defense and commerce.

Both taxation and death may be inevitable, but substantial increases in taxation need not be. Unlike most other Western governments, the government of the United States proved that contention during the post-Eisenhower era.

## The Growth of Government: The Deficit

When people argued that taxes had grown too much in the United States, in the very next breath they often raised the opposite possibility that perhaps taxes had not increased enough. Much criticism was directed at the insidious growth of the federal deficit, which occurs when government spending exceeds tax revenues. The increased size of the deficit purportedly exacerbated inflation and at the same time hampered the ability of the private sector to borrow money to invest and thus create new jobs and improve productivity.

True, the federal government's deficit in the 1970s once climbed to more than $60 billion in a year (in 1976), compared with an average of $3 billion yearly in the 1950s. This amounts to a 20-fold increase, certainly enough to fire talk about the many effects the deficits were thought to have. The total debt of the federal government neared $1 trillion as the post-Eisenhower years closed.

But talk about the deficit in absolute figures, again, ignores proportion. The entire economy had grown. Relative to the size of the economy, the yearly federal deficit remained a small percentage of the GNP in the 1960s and 1970s; in fact, relative to the increase in private borrowing, the rate of growth of the federal deficit was even lower; finally, compared with the deficits of the most competitive economies around the world, including Japan and West Germany, the federal deficits of the 1970s, even at their highest levels, were no different.

Some perspective on the actual increase of the federal deficit can be gained by viewing it in relation to the growth of the whole economy.[16] From 1970 through 1979, the decade of the largest deficits during the post-Eisenhower era, the yearly deficit of the federal government averaged just under 2 percent of GNP, in comparison to about 1 percent of GNP in 1950–60. During the half-decade with the largest deficits, 1975–80, the deficits averaged about 2.5 percent of our GNP, ending the period at about 2 percent of GNP. Although the deficits had grown, they equally remained a relatively small proportion of the GNP over the 1970s, whether one considers the average yearly deficit over the whole decade or that part of the decade with the most pronounced deficits.

A comparison of the increase in the federal deficit with that of the private world is illuminating. Which deficit climbed at a faster rate? "If the American family has to live within its budget, the federal government should learn to do so, too," according to the cliché. When it comes to borrowing money, and increasing one's debt, however, the federal government has been decidedly the junior partner to the American family. During the whole of the period from 1960 through 1979, the federal government increased its debt by a total of $550 billion. Over the same years, the combination of private mortgage and consumer debt, mostly taken on by American families, increased by almost $1.5 trillion.[17] This is not to mention the increase in debt undertaken by the nation's private businesses and industries over that time. After 1960 the federal government increased its debt threefold; the debt assumed by the American family after 1960 grew more than sixfold, a rate of increase in borrowing more than double that of the federal government. Nor was this new, for private debt had also risen rapidly during the 1950s. In fact, if we look at the whole private sector (including corporate business), the rate of increase in private borrowing surpassed that of the government at every point from 1950 to 1980 with the exception of 1974–76. As a result, the federal debt declined as a percentage of total debt in the nation every year, save only two, over the 1950–80 period.

In addition, consider comparative terms.[18] When

compared with even the most economically competitive of other Western nations, the size of the federal government's deficit was not at all unusual. During the 1975–80 period, the years in which the deficit of the United States government rose to its greatest heights, it averaged about 2.5 percent of GNP; yearly governmental deficits averaged around 2.7 percent in West Germany from 1975 until 1979 and about 1.9 percent in Japan. The largest single deficits were 4.8 percent of GNP for West Germany (1975), 4.4 percent of GNP for Japan (1978), and 4.1 percent of GNP for the United States (1976). The deficits of the 1970s in the United States were thus not unlike the deficits found elsewhere in the soundest and most competitive economies of the times.

While I do not claim that the federal deficit had no impact on the economy, neither was the growth of the federal deficit during the post-Eisenhower years monumental, whether in relation to the size of the nation's economy, to the size of the nation's private borrowing, or to the size of the deficits of other competitive nations. And this modest size suggests a moderate overall effect of the deficit on inflation. In 1978 economist George Perry discovered hardly any causal connection between the size of the federal budget deficits of the time and inflation, even allowing such possible influence to reveal itself over a period of four years.[19] Reports from the Congressional Budget Office reinforce the marginal influence of the deficits on inflation during the 1970s.[20] In 1979 the Congressional Budget Office estimated that shaving $25 billion from federal spending, enough then to eliminate much of the deficit, would at best reduce inflation by four-tenths of 1 percent. At the rate of inflation current at the end of 1981, the increase in prices would have declined from 6.8 percent to 6.4 percent. Redoing the analysis in 1980 for the next fiscal year, the Budget Office found again that the budget deficit had only a small effect on the nation's rate of inflation.

## The Growth of Government: The Bureaucracy

The government's capacity to extract economic resources otherwise used in private production goes beyond the power to take money in the form of taxation and deficit spending. Another principal economic resource that the government can command is labor. Labor, translated into government terms, is principally employed to serve in the bureaucracy. Indeed, another of the beliefs that became common in the 1970s involves the feeling that the bureaucracy of government had swelled, that it had expanded well out of proportion relative to the rest of the society and the economy.

It is correct that the number of employees manning the bureaucracy, particularly the state and local bureaucracies, increased throughout the 1960s and 1970s.[21] Government employees (federal, state, and local) rose in number from 8.4 million in 1960 to 15.6 million in 1979. At the same time, it was a period of immensely increasing employment throughout the economy in nonfarm occupations. By 1979, about 89.5 million Americans were employed in nonfarm occupations, compared with fewer than 55 million such employees only two decades earlier in 1960. Examined in proportion to employment, civilian government employees (federal, state, and local) amounted to 15.4 percent of all nonfarm employees in 1960. This percentage was to climb, but only marginally, to 17.4 percent, twenty years later at the conclusion of the 1970s, rising at an annual rate of just about one-tenth of 1 percent a year over the two decades. The rate of expansion in government employment as a proportion of all nonfarm employment was thus moderate. At this rate of growth, even in an additional lifetime, three score and ten years away, governmental employment at all levels would still amount to less than one-quarter of the work force employed in America.

## The Growth of Government: Regulation

An entirely different kind of economic power available to government is the power to regulate the behavior of businesses and individuals. Relative to the size of the economy, the government can take little more, whether in the form of taxes or deficit or manpower, and yet still grow, and grow decisively, by exercising its power to regulate more fully. Regulation in its turn, it is alleged, can greatly sap the economy by way of forcing our industries, businesses, and the public at large to act in uneconomic ways. No taxes or payments to government or increased personnel are necessarily involved, but business and the public bear substantial costs (which they pay in the private market) just to meet and comply with the standards imposed by governmental regulation.

Each year businesses spend billions of dollars to comply with governmental regulatory standards in the consumer and the environmental areas. The cost of an automobile to the consumer increased when the government forced auto companies to install safety belts in cars; the cost to the consumer increased yet again when auto companies were forced to equip each car with emission-control devices. According to Dr. Murray Weidenbaum, who served as President Reagan's first chairman of the Council of Economic Advisers, governmental regulations across all business activities cost government and business and, ultimately, the American taxpayer-consumer more than $100 billion in 1979.[22]

The costs of government in the area of regulation are, to be sure, very difficult to analyze over time, because no overall figures on regulatory costs exist going back into the 1960s or before. Critics who blame exploding regulation for increased costs use detailed evidence about overall costs that cover, for the most part, the 1974–80 period.

No person is more often cited in the discussion and debate about the costs of regulation than Dr. Weidenbaum. Dr. Weidenbaum argues not only that the economic costs of federal regulations on business grew to more that $100 billion in 1979 but that this represents a staggering increase of about $35 billion since 1976 alone [23] and probably amounts to an increase of more than $50 billion since 1974. His findings appear in virtually every kind of publication. They are cited as easily by the president of the United States [24] as by past presidents of the American Economic Association.[25] Companies refer to the findings in their advertising.[26] So widely have Dr. Weidenbaum's figures been reported in popular publications that they seem almost to have acquired the stature of official statistics.

Dr. Weidenbaum's methods of calculation indicated that regulatory costs were 50 percent greater in 1979 than they were in 1976. On this basis, it is not surprising that before 1976 small businesses did not generally perceive government regulations and red tape to be a serious problem. Survey results indicate this conclusion. According to a survey of small businesses taken by the National Federation of Independent Business (NFIB) in 1974, regulation was not then viewed as one of the six most important problems confronting small businesses.[27]

How did Dr. Weidenbaum and his associates arrive at the widely publicized conclusion that federal regulation of business increased by 50 percent between 1976 and 1979 and, likely, 100 percent from 1974 to 1979?[28] His method involves several steps. First, he and his associates determined the "costs of compliance," or how much business pays to conform to government regulations, such as the cost of putting emission controls on automobiles. Compliance costs are so varied across the nation's different businesses and industries, and so terribly complex and time-consuming to uncover, that Dr. Weidenbaum settled on getting detailed answers using 1976 as a single, base year. His work and that of his associates, which also drew on studies carried out by others, estimated the figure for compliance costs to businesses to be about $62 billion for 1976.

The second step involved estimating the federal administrative or bureaucratic costs of regulation, which were derived from the federal budgets of the various regulatory departments and agencies. For 1976, according to Dr. Weidenbaum's estimates, the administrative costs for the various agencies came to about $3.2 billion. To determine the total costs of regulation for 1976, the final step, Dr. Weidenbaum added the government's annual administrative costs of $3.2 billion to the $62 billion in compliance costs paid by business and the consumer, thereby arriving at an overall regulatory burden of about $65 billion for 1976.

Note that the compliance costs of the regulatory burden to business for 1976 ($62 billion) amount to about 20 times the administrative costs ($3.2 billion); on the average, each dollar Congress budgeted in 1976 for administering regulation allegedly produced about a $20 dollar total burden on business to comply with the regulations.

Using this multiplier of 20, Dr. Weidenbaum and his associates calculated the costs of regulation for subsequent years. In 1979 they estimated administrative costs of regulation to be about $4.8 billion, thereby producing an estimated compliance cost of $96 billion ($4.8 billion times 20), and hence an overall regulatory cost of more than $100 billion. Compared with 1976, the overall cost had increased about 55 percent. Thus, his claim that the costs of regulation have skyrocketed might seem to have some justification.

Suppose we use Dr. Weidenbaum's multiplier idea and his own figures on costs: his figures for the administrative and the compliance costs for 1976 and his figures for the administrative costs that compare 1974, 1976, and 1979. His figures for 1976 are presented in Table 1. Dr. Weidenbaum's overall multiplier is found on the bottom line, showing the overall totals. In addition, the right column gives a multiplier (calculated by the author) for each area of regulation used by Dr. Weidenbaum.

As Table 1 indicates, although the overall multiplier

*Table 1.* Costs of Business Regulation, 1976
(in millions of dollars)

| Regulatory area | Administrative cost | Compliance cost | Total | Multiplier[a] |
|---|---|---|---|---|
| Consumer safety and health | $1,516 | $5,094 | $6,610 | 3.5 |
| Job safety | 483 | 4,015 | 4,498 | 8.5 |
| Energy and environment | 612 | 7,760 | 8,372 | 12.5 |
| Financial regulation | 104 | 1,118 | 1,222 | 11.0 |
| Industry-specific | 474 | 26,322 | 26,796 | 55.5 |
| Paperwork | — | 18,000 | 18,000 | — |
| Total | $3,189 | $62,309 | $65,498 | 19.5 |

[a]Compliance cost divided by administrative cost to the nearest 0.5.

*Source:* Murray L. Weidenbaum, "The Costs of Government Regulation of Business," Joint Economic Committee, U.S. Cong., April 10, 1978, p. 16.

for regulation is about 20, the individual multipliers for each regulatory area are vastly different, ranging from 3.5 to 55.5. To draw conclusions based on an overall multiplier, as Dr. Weidenbaum does, is unnecessary. His own research contains more discriminating figures, figures sensitive to the distinctions between very different regulatory areas. It is just as reasonable to employ the appropriate multiplier for each regulatory area and thus allow for the considerable differences that exist.

Table 2 applies the 1976 multipliers shown in Table 1 to the figures Dr. Weidenbaum provides on the annual comparative costs of administering regulation in 1974, 1976, and 1979. It is evident from Table 2 that the single regulatory area with the highest multiplier (industry-specific regulation) had only relatively *low* increases in administrative costs during the period. Indeed, once the appropriate multiplier for each regulatory area is applied to the figures Dr. Weidenbaum supplies, the result differs considerably from the one he announced. Regulatory costs did not increase from 3.8 percent of GNP in 1976 to 4.3 percent of GNP in 1979, as Dr. Weidenbaum would have us believe; instead, such costs remained in fully the same relation with the GNP, staying at 3.2 percent of GNP in both 1976 and 1979.[29] Substantially the same can be said of 1974, the earliest year reported in most of Dr. Weidenbaum's cost studies, when the cost was at 3.1 percent of GNP. In addition, the total cost of federal regulation of business for 1979 amounts to $27 billion less than Dr. Weidenbaum claims. This difference is large: It is almost three times greater than the yearly total value of tax relief first

## Table 2. Costs of Business Regulation,

| Regulatory area | Multiplier | 1974 | | |
| --- | --- | --- | --- | --- |
| | | Administrative cost | Compliance cost | Total |
| Consumer safety and health | 3.5 | $1,302 | $4,557 | $5,859 |
| Job safety | 8.5 | 310 | 2,635 | 2,945 |
| Energy and environment | 12.5 | 347 | 4,338 | 4,685 |
| Financial regulation | 11.0 | 36 | 396 | 432 |
| Industry-specific | 55.5 | 245 | 13,598 | 13,843 |
| Paperwork | — | — | | 16,000 |
| Total | | | | $43,764 |
| GNP | | | | $1,413,000 |
| Total regulatory cost as a % of GNP | | | | 3.1 |
| Total regulatory cost (Weidenbaum) | | | | |
| Total regulatory cost (Weidenbaum) as a % of GNP | | | | |

*Source:* Administrative costs for 1974, 1976, and 1979 are from Murray L. Weidenbaum, "The Costs of Government Regulation of Business," Joint Economic Committee, U.S. Cong., April 10, 1978, p. 12; paperwork costs for 1976 are from the same source, p. 16. Paperwork costs for 1974 and 1979 have been adjusted for inflation, although the Office of Management and Budget estimates that the

1974, 1976, and 1979 (in millions of dollars)

| 1976 | | | 1979 | | |
|---|---|---|---|---|---|
| Adminis-<br>trative<br>cost | Com-<br>pliance<br>cost | Total | Adminis-<br>trative<br>cost | Com-<br>pliance<br>cost | Total |
| $1,613 | $5,646 | $7,259 | $2,671 | $9,349 | $12,020 |
| 446 | 3,791 | 4,237 | 626 | 5,321 | 5,947 |
| 682 | 8,525 | 9,207 | 1,116 | 13,950 | 15,066 |
| 53 | 583 | 636 | 69 | 759 | 828 |
| 270 | 14,985 | 15,255 | 341 | 18,926 | 19,267 |
| | | 18,000 | | | 22,700 |
| | | $54,594 | | | $75,828 |
| | | $1,702,000 | | | $2,368,000 |
| | | 3.2 | | | 3.2 |
| | | $65,498 | | | $102,700 |
| | | 3.8 | | | 4.3 |

burden of paperwork was reduced by 15 percent from 1976 to 1979.
Weidenbaum's total regulatory cost for 1976 is from "The Costs of
Government Regulation of Business," p. 16; Weidenbaum's total
regulatory cost for 1979 is from his *The Future of Government Regulation* (New York: Amacom, 1979), p. 23.

97

proposed for business by the Reagan administration budget. Dr. Weidenbaum's conclusion that the costs of regulation grew at an inordinate rate thus simply vanishes into thin air, and by virtue of none other than the logic of his approach and the figures of his own work.

Allegedly, the climbing cost of governmental regulation placed our industrial power in chains making it difficult for our industries to compete with the growing industrial might of other nations. But regulation in the United States does not appear to have been particularly heavy-handed relative to that of foreign nations. Some comparisons are available from the Organization of European Cooperation and Development in the area of pollution control, the fastest growing area of regulation in the United States during the 1970s. However, despite the increased regulation of the environment in this country, the OECD estimates that regulatory costs for pollution control in Japan as a percentage of the Japanese GNP were even greater and that expenditures in West Germany as a percentage of West German GNP were at least equal to those of the United States.[30] Moreover, to the degree that regulatory costs affected vital areas, such as worker output per hour (known as productivity), the effect appears to have been no greater here than in other Western nations and decidedly less here than in Japan.[31]

Another of the alleged effects of increased regulation is the inflationary pressure it supposedly put on prices. But if, as has been said, the increase in the costs of regulation was small in relation to the size of the economy, then those costs should have played no more than a minor part in the nation's rate of inflation. This is exactly what many economic studies suggest. In the 1970s, Data Resources, Inc., found that the government's environmental controls resulted in a yearly increase of 0.2 percent in the Consumer Price Index; Chase Econometrics calculated that more stringent federal regulation of business produced a yearly increase of 0.4 percent in the Consumer Price Index.[32] These results are fully consistent with the outcome of Dr. Weidenbaum's analysis, when the whole of the logic of his analysis is applied.

With the emphasis of the foregoing discussion having been on the costs of regulation, there perhaps exists some need to remind ourselves that regulation produces a product, whether it be cleaner air and water, or goods that are less hazardous to the consumer, or protection from unscrupulous business and financial practices, or safer conditions in the workplace. Here and in other nations, regulation developed for a reason. Our focus on the costs of regulation should not obscure the many problems, involving a substantial price to the nation, that would likely have surfaced in the wake of the failure to regulate.

## The State of the Economy

Did the American economy founder in the 1970s as a consequence of the growth of the nation's government? It would seem unlikely. One after another, the alleged excessive increases in the burdens the government

99

placed on the backs of the American people have been shown to be not quite the excesses the critics have claimed.

But coupled with this perplexing feature of the 1970s is a complementary one: Despite the common view that the economy was sluggish, the reverse was actually more the truth. Not only did the government not place greater burdens on Americans to the degree so often claimed as the post-Eisenhower years advanced, but neither did the accompanying condition of economic stagnation and decline occur.

We can see this by examining, first, the major elements of economic growth: investment, productivity, and employment. Then we turn to measures of overall growth in the American economy during the post-Eisenhower years: growth in the nation's GNP and growth in real income per American after taxation.

A concern loudly voiced during the 1970s held that increased taxation had made it impossible to garner the funds necessary for an adequate level of investment. Supply side economics grounded itself on the idea that investment had fallen behind, that without investment neither production nor productivity could flourish. All sorts of tax breaks would be necessary to promote the individual and corporate savings needed to rejuvenate investment.

The reader has viewed the evidence that from 1960 to 1980 personal income taxes increased, but not substantially, and that taxes on corporate profits remained relatively constant or actually experienced a decline. Perhaps as a consequence, in no sense did investment decline. As a percentage of the overall economy, investment remained as high in the 1960s and 1970s as it had been in the 1950s.[33] This is so whether one refers to the total of nonresidential investment (such investment amounted to 9.8% of GNP in 1950; 9.5%, in 1960; 10.2%, in 1970; and 10.8%, in 1979) or to investment in new plant and equipment (7.0% of GNP in 1950; 7.2%, in 1960; 8.1% in 1970; and 7.5% in 1979) or to capital purchases in manufacturing industry (1.9% of GNP in 1950; 2.0%, in 1960; 2.3%, in 1970; and 2.5% in 1979) or to the growth in the net stock of fixed nonresidential capital in equipment and structures.[34] Thus, to say that investment had declined, either after 1960 or after 1970, is simply inaccurate. Compared with investment in the 1950s, it had not. Total gross private investment in the nation in 1960 amounted to 15.1 percent of the GNP; by 1979 it had climbed to 16.3 percent.

There also exists some question as to the degree to which productivity declined. The productivity of the American worker has not increased at nearly the rate that productivity has risen in Japan and West Germany. However, the concern was as much that the rate of increase in U.S. productivity had declined, that in fact it had actually halved from rising at a rate of 3.3 percent a year in the 1950s and early 1960s to only 1.7 percent a year from 1972 to 1980. But the American economy of the 1970s was considerably different from that in the 1950s. In the 1950s many more American workers were employed in manufacturing industries relative to workers in the service industries (banking, health care, retail, restaurants). Some part of the change in the nation's productivity is due to this change in occupational mix.

This is easily seen by examining the historical base of our economy, manufacturing, to which the critics presumably refer when they debate the need to reinvigorate the economy by "reindustrializing America." How has manufacturing productivity fared in the United States?[35] From 1950 to 1960, the average increase in the productivity of American workers in manufacturing industries was 2.4 percent a year; this was followed by an unusual period, 1960–65, in which productivity increased almost 5 percent a year (leading to an average for the 1950–65 period of about 3.5 percent). The 1965–70 period, on the other hand, saw only small productivity increases in manufacturing of about 1.2 percent a year. Productivity in American manufacturing then rose in the 1970s, climbing to levels that surpassed those of the 1950s. An average increase in manufacturing productivity of about 2.7 percent a year took place from 1970 through 1979 compared with an increase of 2.4 percent a year from 1950 to 1960.[36] With the exception of the brief and wholly abnormal period of 1960–65, productivity increases during the 1970s in American manufacturing were as vigorous as, indeed somewhat stronger than, they had been at any time from 1950 onward. Nor was there any deterioration in our manufacturing trade balance with foreign countries.[37]

Another crucial factor behind economic growth is labor. During the post-Eisenhower years, the number of gainfully employed Americans mushroomed.[38] From 1960 to 1980 the economy added more than 30 million jobs, thereby leading to an increase in total employment of practically 50 percent in that one generation alone. During the last half of the 1970s, the yearly percentage increase in the total number of employed people almost doubled that of any other period since World War II and was *four* times greater than the percentage increase of the 1950s. Literally 12 million new jobs were created and filled in the five years between 1975 and 1980 compared with less than 7 million during the entire decade of the 1950s.[39]

As the foregoing facts suggest, and completely contrary to the image coming out of the 1970s, a vigorous expansion of the nation's economy occurred throughout much of the post-Eisenhower era. Few argue with the nation's record of unparalleled economic success during the 1960s. During the 1960s, both the gross national product after adjusting for inflation and the Industrial Production Index of the nation rose by about 50 percent. What is far less understood and appreciated is the degree to which the growth of the economy stretched out across the 1970s. Again, let us turn to the 1950s as a point of comparison. The increase in the real gross national product, after adjusting for inflation, was fully as great during the 1970s (3.7 percent yearly) as in the 1950s (3.5 percent yearly).[40] The nation's Industrial Production Index climbed quickly, too. In fact, expanding by nearly half, industrial production rose at a faster rate in the United States during the 1970s than it did in any major West European nation, including West Germany and France, and rose only slightly less than it did in Japan.[41]

Consequently, personal income increased quite rapidly in the United States during the 1970s, as well as during the 1960s.[42] Real disposable income (after subtracting for both inflation and taxes) climbed as quickly in the 1970s as in the 1950s; indeed, because the growth rate of the American population was lower in the 1970s, real disposable income per *individual* American actually rose almost twice as rapidly in the 1970s as in the 1950s. After adjusting for inflation and taxes, income in the United States rose from $2,386 per American in 1950 to $2,697 per American in 1960, an increase of 13 percent. From 1970 through 1979, after adjusting for inflation and taxes, Americans registered a 24.7 percent increase in income per person, from $3,619 to $4,512. In the entire two-decade period, 1960–80, the growth in real, spendable income per American was truly remarkable, reaching to 60 percent.

Considering both the degree and the duration of the economy's expansion in the post-Eisenhower years, one is not surprised by the immense growth that occurred in the ownership of a whole series of products over the period. For example, in the final fifteen years of the post-Eisenhower era, from 1965 through 1979, the proportion of American families owning air conditioners rose by 30 percent; those owning clothes dryers rose by 34 percent; color television sets, 66 percent; food waste disposals, 26 percent; ranges, 31 percent; and a 50 percent increase took place in the number of automobiles on the American roads.[43] The proportion of families owning their own homes also climbed to new highs in the 1960s and rose again in the 1970s. By the end of the 1970s two-thirds of all American families had their own homes, the highest percentage of the twentieth century.[44] Between 1973 and 1980 the number of homes owned by Americans increased by 15 percent. Both decades of the post-Eisenhower years witnessed potent economic growth, bringing great advances in material well-being to ever-larger percentages of Americans, just as had earlier characterized the 1950s.

## *Conclusion*

President Reagan told the American people, and many economists and politicians of the day came substantially to agree, that the government was no longer the answer to the nation's economic problems but instead had become an important part of the problems. But in what way was government a serious element of the problem? Income taxes had grown very little for most Americans between 1960 and 1980 in relation to the growth in personal income; property taxes had stayed about the same relative to personal income over the period; corporate-profits taxes, too, had remained broadly constant, and in some respects had even declined; the budget deficit rose modestly in relation to GNP over the 1960–80 period and at its highest level was not unlike the deficits in Japan and West Germany; the numbers of people employed in the government bureaucracies had grown very little relative to the numbers employed elsewhere in the American economy in nonfarm occupations; nor is there much evidence that the costs of government regulation of business increasingly took a larger part of the economic pie as the 1970s progressed or that regulatory costs were greater in the United States than in other economically competitive nations.

As these conclusions all seem to argue that government was not responsible for the ever-growing burden on the American taxpayer and economy, what did cause the economic ills facing the nation? According to the common presupposition, "Everywhere America has looked, it has seen the symptoms of its economic impasse . . ."[45] In point of fact, however, neither the symptoms nor the ills were quite what we had been led to believe. Instead, the real GNP grew vigorously in the 1970s and investment in the nation's businesses and industries remained strong relative to the GNP; employment exploded in the 1970s, and manufacturing productivity rose at no less than its normal rate; industrial production climbed at a fast pace, faster than the growth of production of nearly all other major Western industrialized nations over the 1970s[46]; in fact, the rate of increase in real, spendable income for the average American (after subtracting for inflation and taxes) climbed faster during the 1970s than in the 1950s.

How, then, did so many Americans ever come to believe the reverse of all these conclusions? What led to the view that government had grown uncontrollably when it had not? How did we come to see the economy as failing when it was not? I turn next to these puzzling and troublesome questions.

# 4

How False Images Became
Accepted Doctrine

THE POST-EISENHOWER YEARS evolved into an era of
widespread misconception about the quality of the nation's governance. By every standard guiding the discussions in the preceding chapters, illusions about the
government increasingly gripped the nation. In turn,
these illusions contributed to the development of a new
popular consensus, a consensus that drew upon an almost obsessive criticism of government. By the end of
the post-Eisenhower years, the philosophy that advocated a strong, active government, which had coun-
seled the nation in the immediate past, had been
thoroughly discredited. In its place, the ideas behind the
advancing new consensus catapulted to power.

The emergence of the many illusions raises troubling
questions. What persuaded the American public to accept with such seeming alacrity the devastating critique
found in the main premises of the new consensus? Con-

sider, for example, the claim that the size of the public sector had grown at dangerous speed over the post-Eisenhower era. What gave this general view its irresistible appeal? Or the notion that the government's expanding social programs had contributed little of vital significance to the nation's well-being? Consider the economy, too. How could we have come to think during the 1970s that the economy was foundering, drifting listlessly, when it was actually experiencing one of the longest surges of sustained growth in production during peacetime since 1918? No shortage of positive facts existed to counter the emerging new consensus. Why, then, did all these facts remain obscure, so obscure that no other viewpoint proved even slightly worthy of public notice? To discover the causes of the many illusions of the day is crucial. For in becoming aware of the sources of our excessive negativism, we learn why the new consensus was able to assume command and to crush the public philosophy that had guided and served us in the past.

## The Rise of the New Conservatism

Obviously, the government made its own share of tragic mistakes during the post-Eisenhower years, most notably Vietnam and Watergate. For eight years, at the very heart of the post-Eisenhower era, these episodes stood uppermost in Americans' minds. The precipitous decline of the public's confidence in government arose as opposition began to mount against the war in Vietnam. Both Vietnam and Watergate contributed decisively to the spiraling growth of mistrust in government that came about during those years.

It should be understood that Vietnam and Watergate developed as they did partly because the normal political processes had been largely cast aside. More so than most issues of the post-Eisenhower decades, Vietnam and Watergate were characterized by a highly centralized decision-making process instead of the usual more decentralized method that allows the checks and balances of government to operate; by a closed and secretive, rather than an open, process of decision; and by command rather than by full debate. Both episodes ended in great misfortune for the nation as well as for the political officials involved. This being so, the episodes might (and I think should) have eventually worked to heighten popular appreciation and to restore respect for the more decentralized and open ways by which the nation's government usually carried out its business, given the back-to-back tragedies that occurred in their absence. Why did this not happen? Possibly because, in the twilight of the Vietnam and Watergate experiences, other powerfully unsettling problems took their place for which the public did hold the usual processes of politics accountable.

At their furthest extension, Vietnam and Watergate lasted through 1975, whereas the public's disillusionment with government continued virtually unabated thereafter, in many respects becoming more widespread by the end of the post-Eisenhower years.[1] Although Vietnam and Watergate exercised profound influence, neither can fully explain why the public's confidence failed to replenish even to a degree after 1975 but instead eroded yet further. Alongside Vietnam and Watergate, negative reaction to the country's economic situation during the 1970s also had a good deal to do with how people felt about government. Reinforcing and even exacerbating the change of opinion toward government that began with Vietnam and Watergate, the economic problems facing the nation—those of high unemployment and inflation—came increasingly to the fore, eventually dominating the nation's debate by the end of the post-Eisenhower era. The problems besetting the economy seemed without cure.

People's outlooks about many matters, including politics, are influenced to some degree by their economic outlook.[2] The nation's economic performance throughout the 1970s witnessed something new: the simultaneous increase of both unemployment and inflation, a phenomenon that came to be known as stagflation. Stagflation persisted, seemingly endlessly. The very word "stagflation" aroused images of a weakened, listing economy on the verge of sinking. None of the policies initiated by the government to rectify the rising levels of unemployment and inflation appeared to work. Into this context slipped an ideology that, by the end of the post-Eisenhower years, became the linchpin of the new consensus. The ideology keyed on the public's image of a failing economy, which arose in good part from that very sign of failure, the onset and persistence of stagflation. In addition, the new ideology played on the popular image of an inept and ineffectual government, which also stemmed partly from the onset of stagflation and the government's apparent inability to end it. Since popular confidence in government was weak—in fact, at a miserable low—the next step was indeed simple: the new ideology identified the signal cause of the growing unemployment and inflation as the government itself.

In advancing this premise, the spokesmen for the gathering new consensus contended that the government's disinclination to curb its own growth—its unwillingness to restrain the ever-tightening grip of taxation, deficits, bureaucracy, regulation, and waste—now stood as a principal economic problem of the time. The totality of all these aspects of expanding governmental intrusion had created such heavy financial burdens and had cost the economy so much, it was claimed, that prices spiraled ever upward while the formation of new jobs was greatly slowed. Under the massive weight of governmental intervention, the competitive mechanisms that balance the free market no longer worked properly. Additionally, the public sector's wild growth had drained vast monies away from private investment, further impeding the capacity of the economy to create new jobs and to improve productivity. With all this in mind, the conclusion followed confidently that one action alone could effectively redress the nation's deepening economic problems. To rectify unemployment, inflation, declining investment, and slowed productivity growth, the failed policies of the past, and with them the government's expansion in all its forms, had to be turned around.[3]

One important element of these newly fashionable

views stood the test of evidence. Although the growth in manufacturing productivity advanced normally during the post-Eisenhower years as compared with earlier years, this was not the case in other parts of the economy, particularly in the service areas. In these areas, progress in improving productivity declined to a disconcerting degree throughout the 1970s, a matter to which I will return later.

However, most of the remaining ideas underlying the new consensus bore little resemblance to the evidence, and, surprisingly, this made hardly any difference.[4] It seemed not to matter, for example, that relative to the size of the economy, the revenues available to the public sector had risen very little over the last decade of the era (far less, in fact, than in most other major Western nations with which we competed economically), or that the federal income tax bite in the United States amounted to little more in the 1960s and 1970s as a percentage of income than it had at the close of the 1950s, or that the size of the bureaucracy in proportion to the employed work force had risen only marginally after 1960, or that governmental regulation had probably neither grown as disproportionately as alleged nor placed the nation at the internationally competitive disadvantage that was claimed. These considerations, as well as the many other evidences that the burdens of the public sector were considerably more confined than the impressions conveyed, seemed to matter little.

On the other hand, if evidence about the public sector's confined growth was insufficient to change minds, perhaps facts about business investment in the United

States would. A major argument blamed a decline in business investment on the government's unbridled growth. Again, the evidence said otherwise, for in fact no decline in the nation's rate of business investment— gross or net—took place in the United States during the 1970s or the 1960s.

Nor, finally, had the economy diminished in its power to bring new employment into being, as the arguments behind the evolving new consensus frequently intimated. Quite the opposite. During the post-Eisenhower years new employment opportunities for Americans had been fashioned at a rate far in excess of prior years. Yet this, too, failed to muffle the voices that were building the new consensus.

## A Vacuum of Ideas

If they often lacked accuracy, however, the arguments that eventually won power did enjoy a prized asset. They were supported by vast sums of money. After stagflation's appearance, many corporations and other producer interests expended vast amounts of money pounding the new arguments home. Almost daily, these interests publicized allegation after allegation about the negative economic effects of the size, power, and inefficiencies of government. They did so through television, newspaper, and magazine advertising, by way of think-tank publications, and in political-action committee advertising on behalf of favored candidates. The leaders who advanced the new arguments used every conceivable outlet.

But, to account for the popularity of the arguments, enormous sums of money, while important, provide an insufficient explanation, for plenty of money was available from other quarters to publicize other ideas. Instead, crucial to their success, the arguments evolved at a time when there existed few other ideas, a virtual vacuum of thought, with liberal views in almost complete disarray. The liberals, reeling in self-doubt, could neither explain nor provide a solution to stagflation. Gripped by concern over stagflation, many Americans began to search for some new direction of action and willingly considered almost any direction other than the policies and the programs that had dominated the past. Few knew what to think. The new ideology entered into this void.

In the absence of a coherent counterview, proponents of the new ideology easily cultivated the myth of a floundering economy. They needed only to refer to the seemingly perpetual conditions of increasing unemployment and inflation, sure signs of economic decline. Never mind the contradictory evidence. Never mind that throughout the 1970s unequaled numbers of new jobs had been created and that by any measure the nation's economic output had grown vigorously. Critics could ignore these inconvenient facts about the nation's economic performance. They could ignore the fact that rates of investment had not declined and the evidence that the relative levels of personal income taxation, regulation, and most other forms of governmental intervention had changed little. All these contradictory facts could be ignored because, amid the unusual economic times, the opposition, the liberals, provided no coherent ideas of their own to serve the public as an alternative focus of debate. Facts to contradict the new ideology were there, the means to focus those facts was not.

## The Crowded Generation

Some other powerful forces, which have thus far eluded us, are needed to help explain all the illusions and contradictions of the times. They must stand aside from the various and sundry alleged faults in America's past governance to which the critics had successfully directed the nation's attention. Because Americans were easily attracted to the critic's claims about our flawed governance during the past, however, these other powerful forces must have worked something like an optical illusion to distort our vision of the government and the economy. They must have twisted the images we received in much the manner as does water in causing us to see a perfectly straight object as sharply bent when the object passes through the liquid's surface.

Certainly the government's own rhetoric at the start in overselling its programs was a factor of some importance. In making excessive claims about what the programs could accomplish, the government undoubtedly created expectations that later contributed to the programs' fall from grace. Still, even this consideration remains secondary. Far more important, the true performances of the government and the economy over the post-Eisenhower years escaped view because of our failure to recognize and appreciate the full implications of the underlying conditions of the times. The conditions facing the post-Eisenhower years framed a fundamental issue that the era was required to address. This vital issue had to do with a series of quiet forces whose towering effects would be to swell the nation's labor supply enormously throughout the whole of the post-Eisenhower years following 1965. One of the key economic questions facing the era, and upon which the nation's attention and debate should have been fixed far more than it was, concerned precisely how the nation should respond to this brutal series of forces. Unhappily, although discussed in some circles,[5] the issue never reached anything approaching a central theme of political dialogue or the everyday notice of the public that it needed and deserved.

A crucial circumstance of the post-Eisenhower years was the crushing avalanche of American workers entering the labor market. From 1965 to 1980, the nation's work force grew by 40 percent, swelling by almost 30 million workers. The American people were certainly burdened and the economy was certainly in torment, but the culprit was not the government. It was, paradoxically, the people themselves.

Simple figures here tell a lot. Every society's economy needs to prepare a place for the new generation entering adulthood. In the 1950s the economy of the Eisenhower years had to prepare places for the generation entering adulthood, a generation that had been born in the 1930s.[6] The members of the new generation would need jobs providing enough income to make a decent living. The birth rate in the 1930s was about 18 to 19 per 1,000 adults. In contrast to this, the late 1960s and the 1970s had to address the needs for jobs and income of people born and raised from 1945 to 1960. This generation's birth rate averaged 24.2 per 1,000 adults throughout the 1945–60 period, a rate approximately one-third greater than in the 1930s. About 59 million Americans were born from 1946 through 1960, and about 61 million from 1951 through 1965. This compares to the births of about 39 million Americans, or 22 million fewer, between 1931 and 1945.

In addition to the mounting population coming of age during the post-Eisenhower years, the attitude among women, especially among women under the age of 45, toward entering the work force changed. One indication of this changed attitude is found in the decision of women to attend college: Whereas in 1960 only about 18 percent of female high school graduates entered college, by 1975 about 30 percent did, approaching closely the rate for male high school graduates. Increasingly, young women would want and feel that they deserved jobs, both in numbers and proportions not seen in prior years. Furthermore, the rate in the dissolution of marriages greatly increased in the late 1960s and the 1970s, placing still more people in need of jobs. From 1970 to 1980 the rate of divorce almost doubled that of 1950–60.[7]

These three developments—the vastly increased numbers of births from the late 1940s through the mid-1960s, the changed attitudes toward employment among women, and the increased rates of divorce in the late 1960s and 1970s—acted in combination to place tens of millions of new people in search of jobs after 1965. Taken all together, the three developments hitting the post-Eisenhower era could easily place 45 million to 50 million new young adults in the labor market, or a net increase of up to 25 million workers, after subtracting for other workers who would normally retire. Then, on top of this, the mass of people entering the work force would create its own effect: Numbers of other young families, to keep pace (given the depressed wages resulting from the increased competition for jobs), would themselves send a second earner into the job market. The total effect was extraordinary. In 1965, five years after the start of the post-Eisenhower era, the nation's labor force numbered just under 75 million Americans.[8] By the end of 1979, the labor force had mushroomed to about 104 million Americans, an increase of about 30 million. These very large numbers carried something of the force of a tidal wave. Above and beyond the 12 million Americans who came into the labor force from 1950–65, almost two and one-half times that many entered the labor force in 1965–80. In the fifteen years following 1965, the immense growth in the numbers of workers—29 million—amounted to more than half the entire labor force of Japan or, indeed, surpassed the total labor force of either France or West Germany. To avoid massive unemployment, new jobs would have to be created at a decisively faster pace after 1965 than in the 1950–65 period. Not even a modestly faster pace would do, for the growth in the number of Americans seeking employment after 1965 would far exceed that of the earlier period.

No other major Western economy—neither Japan, West Germany, France, nor Britain—had to contend with this titanic expansion of the work force. None of these nations experienced an escalating birth rate approaching that in the United States in 1945–65;[9] none experienced an increase in the work force approaching that in the United States in 1965–80. West Germany recorded no increase at all in the size of its labor force over the decade of the 1970s. During the 1970s, in fact, Japan's labor force recorded the largest single increase of all the major Western nations aside from the United States: It amounted to a healthy expansion of about 9 percent, just about one-third the percentage increase in American job seekers over those years.[10] In facing the circumstance of vast numbers of people seeking jobs, the United States was thus *unique* among major industrialized nations. The people who entered the work force in America from 1965 onward rightly deserve to be called "the crowded generation."

This burst of people entering the job market shocked the nation's economy. The job market could not possibly absorb all the job seekers, especially the young who constituted much of the crowded generation. Young or not, however, unemployed and employed Americans were more similar than dissimilar: Among the workers who would become unemployed, the large majority were *not* a second earner in the family but the main breadwinner. An extensive survey of unemployed Americans in 1976 found that 65 percent of the unemployed at that time were the family's main wage earner and that three in ten were both the main wage earner

119

and had children.[11] In these characteristics, the unemployed were not vastly different from the employed: 74 percent of the employed in 1976 were the family's main wage earner and four in ten were both the main wage earner and had children.[12]

If unemployment would likely grow with the pronounced swell of job seekers, there remained only the question of how much. Awesome possibilities loomed. Had the rate of job creation achieved in the halcyon days of 1950–65 been fully sustained over 1965–80, without change, unemployment by the middle of 1980 would have stood somewhere around 18 million Americans, or about 17 percent of the labor force;[13] unemployment among Americans under the age of 35 could easily have exceeded 25 percent, possibly 30 percent, with little prospect of employment over the long term. Nothing approaching these awful, depressionlike conditions took place for two reasons. First, because of the expansion of both social security and other benefits for the elderly, greater numbers of senior citizens could afford to retire at age 65, thereby opening up these jobs to the young. In 1980 only 15 percent of Americans over the age of 65 were employed, compared with about 25 percent just two decades earlier. Second, remarkably, new employment was fashioned at an unsurpassed rate in 1965–80, a rate almost double that of the period from 1950–65. But even 25 million new jobs, a truly superlative effort, were not fully satisfactory, given the onslaught of the crowded generation. While unemployment did not surge to 15 or 17 percent by 1980, it did rise from about 4 percent in 1965 to just over 7 percent in 1980.

The story begins to gain focus. Even if the nation had created and filled unequaled numbers of new jobs after 1965, which it did; and even if the nation's business investment had grown at fully normal levels, which it did; and even if, as the result of the climb in employment and investment, the nation's industrial production and its income after inflation grew vigorously, which they did; even if all of these happened, which they all did, the rate of unemployment in the United States would still rise to about 7 percent at the end of the post-Eisenhower years. The numbers of job seekers were that vast.

Nor was the extraordinary pace of job creation achieved without cost. The jobs were generated in large measure by the private sector, not by public employment or some other form of sweeping governmental intervention. However, to accelerate the private sector's creation of new jobs, demand in the economy would need to be maintained at a high level. This important ingredient, an expansion in demand, originated following 1965 partly by way of a rise in net borrowing. The majority of this rise came from borrowing within the private sector, whose growth eclipsed that of public sector borrowing.[14] Creating still more demand was a second crucial factor: the relation between real wages and productivity.[15] Between 1965 and 1970, the real wages of the American worker climbed faster, by more than 3 percent, than did the growth in workers' productivity. Wages rose in this manner not as the result of unreasonable demands by labor; rather, the rise in wages simply made up for earlier losses, reflecting en-

121

tirely a lag from the earlier 1960–65 period when the reverse had been the case. Between 1960 and 1965 the productivity of employees had climbed fully 7 percent more than did their real wages. The twin effects of the growth in net (mostly private) borrowing after 1965 and the rise in workers' wages relative to productivity (to compensate for earlier years) joined together to increase demand after 1965, which, in turn, put a greater inflationary pressure on prices in the 1965–70 period than had been the case during the 1960–65 period. These factors, both originating largely from within the private sector, helped condition the rising rate of inflation that began after 1965.

As demand began to rise, the government could have chosen a policy of not permitting the money supply to expand beyond prior rates of increase. Yet as demand in the economy heated, a necessary condition if the private sector was to bring new jobs into being at unprecedented speed, the potential of an unemployment rate among Americans of 14, 15, or even 17 percent still lay down the road. No matter the number of new jobs created this year, or the previous year, either. The crowded generation would continue to swell the labor market. Each year, year after year, over the whole period following 1965, the crowded generation would sustain the march. To avoid massive unemployment, the economy would have to continue fashioning new jobs at a markedly accelerated pace. Any domestic policy to contain prices would have to reckon with the immense numbers of unemployed that would surely follow if sustained efforts were made to clamp down on demand

and slow the economy. In the circumstance, a nightmarish balancing act was required in which the best result obtainable (unless the government itself directly created many more of the new jobs, and even this is far from certain) would likely involve some increase in unemployment and some increase in demand and hence prices, all taking place together. Enter stagflation.

Moreover, any policy undertaken by the government would be exposed to additional inflationary blows that might hit from elsewhere. From 1965 through 1972, the year before the economy first experienced stiff international oil price hikes, inflation in the United States generally hovered between 4 and 5 percent.[16] But in the face of a series of external shocks—especially the sharp rise in energy prices in the winter of 1973 and in 1974 and again in 1979–80—the American government could employ strong deflationary policies in the manner of some of its major economic competitors, such as West Germany, only if we were prepared to incur far greater increases in unemployment. For not one of the other major Western countries faced the exceptionally large numbers of people entering into its labor force. Thus, from 1973 through 1980, the rate of inflation in the United States went above 10 percent during three of the five years in which world energy prices rose sharply.[17] In every other year, inflation remained within single figures; in fact, in only one of these post-Eisenhower years did inflation rise above 7 percent. The average rate of inflation during the final three years that escaped international petroleum price increases—1976 through 1978—registered slightly under 7 percent.

So the huge crowds moving into the American labor market had a double effect: First, they guaranteed a rise in the unemployment rate almost regardless of the action of the American government and economy; second, they narrowed the options that the government had available to deal with inflation. To stimulate demand to permit the creation of jobs at double the usual rate by the private market would cause some upward pressure on prices. Then, during five of the eight years from 1973 through 1980, the pressure on prices would further intensify because of the stiff oil price increases and other external circumstances. After 1965, unemployment and inflation together, stagflation, would become a recurring feature of the post-Eisenhower economy. Yet even in the face of stagflation, other fundamental sectors of the economy—business investment, employment, industrial production, gross national output, and real income after inflation—forged ahead at very healthy rates of increase compared with the Eisenhower years. In each of these vital respects, the American economy was by no means failing. It was strong.

And this stands as a vital point, a point we must understand about the economic conditions of those years. Neither the unemployment nor the inflation of the post-Eisenhower era derived essentially from a failing economy, nor from economic ills brought to pass by an allegedly overgrown government, for the economy's performance had been strong. To a larger degree than is presently recognized, stagflation emerged instead from the need to address the demanding challenges of the crowded generation, challenges that had been made even more complicated by the exceptional energy price increases of those times.

Nor did the influence of the crowded generation end there. As important, the crowded generation would also frustrate efforts after 1965 to raise the productivity of American workers (the output per worker per hour of labor). Whereas productivity in American manufacturing continued to move ahead at relatively normal rates during most of the post-Eisenhower era, other economic sectors did not fare as well, particularly the service sectors, where productivity growth slowed dramatically. The decline in productivity growth did not result from a decline in business investment, because such investment ran at fairly normal levels over both decades of the post-Eisenhower era. Productivity within the service sectors slowed, in part, because a vast proportion of the 25 million new jobs created over these years were precisely in those sectors.[18] Because of the large rise in jobs, the total investment relative to the numbers employed had to diminish even if investment continued to climb at normal rates of growth. Given the dramatically increased number of employees, a lower ratio of capital to labor resulted over the period. According to some estimates, this factor may account for up to 60 percent of the decline in the nation's productivity that occurred following 1973.[19] Moreover, still another consequence of the crowded generation would function to depress workers' productivity. As the young and inexperienced workers of the crowded generation flooded the labor market, their proportion of the employed work force relative to older, more seasoned workers would likewise increase. The rate of substitution of persons below the age of 25 for those over 55 in the work force doubled after 1965.[20] The substitution of younger, less experienced people in managerial positions was also pronounced. Economist Mark Perlman points out: "The comparative youthfulness of the labor force in the 1970s, compounded by the analogous 'youthening' of the supervisory workers . . . certainly seems to offer a prima facie reason for the decline in worker output."[21] Other estimates indicate that the change in the age composition of the work force may account for one-quarter to one-third of the decline in productivity in 1966–73, although somewhat less thereafter.[22] Economists constantly wonder about which factors to hold responsible for upward or downward movements in productivity. Although no single or even dominant explanation exists, as a former deputy director of the Office of Management and Budget pointed out,[23] most studies indicate that the nation's productivity from 1965 to 1973 was negatively affected by the change in the age composition of the labor force, and that a diminution of the capital–labor ratio further contributed to the reduction of productivity following 1973.

## The Failure to Understand

Despite its implications for our levels of unemployment, inflation, and productivity, the onset of the crowded generation, as an issue to be addressed, only rarely took center stage in the nation's political debate. The debate on the economy between Republicans and

Democrats, and between liberals and conservatives, often flitted about it, but the focus remained on the relative merits of Keynes, traditional conservative balanced-budget theories, and the new supply-side economics. The underlying context of the crowded generation, into which any economic theory needed to be placed in order to understand the theory's true meaning and relative merits, was often left in the shadows outside the spotlight of attention.

That this is so is perplexing and deservedly a matter of study in itself: How could such developments, so crucial to the economic affairs of the nation for the better part of a generation, remain, for the most part, at the outer edge of political discussion? Numerous answers suggest themselves, some combination of which probably constitutes a proper explanation. For one, the Vietnam and Watergate experiences had monopolized the nation's attention until the pressures of the crowded generation were already well upon us. Even were this not so, by reducing the credibility of elected officials, these episodes would have made it more difficult in any case for political leaders to develop and articulate points of view about issues that the public would accept at face value. For another, few leaders seemed to want to focus the public's attention on the issues connected to the crowded generation. Perhaps the liberals left a vacuum in this regard because their economics had seemingly worked well for a generation or longer. The New Deal and then the New Frontier were both proclaimed economic successes. Knowingly or not, both employed the concept that a change in the level of demand is at the same time the root problem and the great cure of economics. Immersed in the conventional concepts of Keynesian economics, is it possible that liberals could not bring into focus the new reality that the root problem was no longer mainly demand but an oversupply of labor? If so, no wonder liberal rhetoric increasingly appeared to be answers to problems long past. Or perhaps, unlike supply-side economics, economic ideas centering on the impending oversupply of labor could not be "packaged" in sufficiently simple terms to communicate them properly through the media. Still another possibility is that no one dared to communicate the future reality. Supply-side speakers at the close of the 1970s promised a reduction in both inflation and unemployment, a pleasant promise to make and a blessing to hear. Any message conveyed during the post-Eisenhower years by a person conscious of the powerful economic effects and aftermath of the crowded generation would be far less optimistic. Both unemployment and inflation would have to go up at least a degree to provide a place for the new generation of Americans entering the labor market. Either that or the government itself would have to create many more millions of jobs or exercise some other form of massive intervention. Not an easy theme to deliver and survive.

The main fault in the nation's governance lay not especially in any of the particulars for which it was so roundly criticized at the close of the 1970s: It lay not in the degree to which the public sector grew or in any absence of value of the domestic programs. Rather, the main fault in the end was the failure, probably for a variety of reasons, to impress upon the public the essential context within which the economy and government were called upon to operate and by which the public should measure their success. Neither Democrats nor Republicans, liberals nor conservatives, adequately directed the public's attention to the crowded generation or to the towering economic challenges it portended. And because the context was poorly understood, the degree to which the post-Eisenhower era succeeded in handling the difficult circumstances of the day produced the image not of success but of failure.

## *Hidden Success*

The opposite also holds. To appreciate the context of the times enables one to recognize the success of the nation in managing the economic situation it faced. By all counts, unemployment in the United States should have grown by leaps and bounds as the crowded generation surged into the labor market. Despite this, the nation's rate of unemployment for 1980 (7.1 percent) stood less than two points higher than it did in 1960 (5.5 percent), the final year of Eisenhower's term of office. By the end of the post-Eisenhower years, miraculously, no massive rise had taken place in the nation's unemployment rate. Potentially, more than 10 million Americans had been spared joblessness—in most cases long-term joblessness—with the multitude of personal hardships and societal costs that joblessness is known to entail. To accommodate the millions who spilled into the American labor force after 1965 was no simple task.

As we have seen, it took a record performance in creating new jobs. Even during the fifteen most difficult years, those years following 1965, the nation's unemployment grew by only half, from 4.5 percent of the American labor force in 1965 to 7.1 percent in 1980. In containing the climb of the unemployment rate to about half during those years, the nation achieved a record that neither Japan, nor West Germany, nor France, nor Britain surpassed, or in most cases even equaled (Table 3). Yet not one of these other nations faced the crowded generation of the 1965–80 years that was found here. The American performance was truly remarkable and might well have been the cause of celebration. But few of us thought more than casually about the challenge set

*Table 3.* Rate of Unemployment and Changes in Rates of Unemployment, Major Western Nations, 1965 and 1980

|  | Rate of unemployment | | Change in rate of unemployment | |
|---|---|---|---|---|
|  | *1965* | *1980* | *Absolute increase* | *Percentage rate of increase* |
| United States | 4.5 | 7.1 | 2.6 | 58 |
| Japan | 1.2 | 2.0 | 0.8 | 67 |
| United Kingdom | 2.1 | 7.4 | 5.3 | 252 |
| France | 1.4 | 6.5 | 5.1 | 364 |
| West Germany | 0.3 | 3.0 | 2.7 | 900 |

*Source: Economic Report of the President,* (Washington, D.C.: U.S. Government Printing Office, 1982), p. 357, Table B-111.

by the crowded generation for the nation, so few of us celebrated the achievement.

To accomplish this marvelous result, the economy of the post-Eisenhower years had to grow vigorously. Even the decade of the 1950s failed to overshadow the rate of income growth after inflation that took place during either the 1960s or the 1970s. In both decades, too, the nation's overall production climbed in a manner either comparable to, or faster than, the 1950s.

But if the nation's income growth *after inflation* was really so high, and continued throughout the 1970s, something confounding requires explanation. Why did the much-reported median income of the American family not also rise rapidly, but instead only inch forward during the 1970s? The answer lies once more in the effects of the crowded generation. Both in the late 1960s and during the 1970s, massive numbers of Americans entered into adulthood, leading to the formation of large numbers of new households. In addition, many more Americans became willing to live singly. As a result, the growth of income in America would be divided among far larger numbers of individual living units (families plus unrelated individuals, using census terminology) than had been so during earlier times. The number of families plus unrelated individuals climbed by 24 million from 1965 through 1979, compared with about 12 million in 1950–65.[24] It was not so much that the economic pie was shrinking, but rather that it was being shared among larger numbers. Moreover, because families in the 1970s were increasingly headed by females, by the young, and by senior citizens, most of the units composing the burgeoning numbers fell into the lower half of the income scale. With income divided among so many and with a high percentage of the expanding numbers coming from economic groups in the lower half of the income scale, the median income could not advance forward at a rate comparable to the rapid growth of the larger economy. Under the circumstances of the crowded generation, it was an accomplishment that the median family income advanced forward at all, an accomplishment made possible only because of the potent growth of the economy after inflation both in the 1960s and the 1970s, growth as vibrant as that of the 1950s.

Nor is there serious doubt that the policies of the post-Eisenhower years contributed decisively to reducing the percentage of Americans living in poverty by 50 percent or more, or that the private economy could not have approached the impact that the government's programs demonstrated in this vital concern. An unfettered free-market economy sounds nice in theory. But in the context of the crowded labor markets and intense competition for jobs, even a vigorously expanding private market was incapable of reaching large numbers from the weaker economic groups who were living in poverty. The government's social programs of the post-Eisenhower years could reduce poverty where the private economy could not, and the programs accomplished this reduction. Beyond that, the programs could do no more. They could not hope to give recipients a fully firm footing outside the continuation of transfer payments in an economy burdened by surplus labor and a fierce competition for jobs. This set the stage for still another extraordinary irony. Despite the successes of the social programs when compared to the record of the private sector, these programs would nevertheless come to seem ineffective and wasteful partly because of their perpetual need for enlarged funding and partly because unemployment continued to climb. Claims that the private sector could do much better ran apace. Not much understood was the message of the actual record, which said the very reverse.

In addition to reducing the percentage of Americans who lived in poverty by more than half, the government's social programs prevented a marked and perhaps intolerable increase in the gap between the economically stronger and weaker groups of Americans. As the labor surplus mounted, large numbers of Americans, particularly those from the traditionally weaker economic groups—young persons, people with low levels of education, women, and the elderly— would have difficulty staying above water. Amid the competition, the better jobs would be snapped up by person after person in the long lines of applicants from the stronger economic groups, leaving no jobs or the lowest-paying jobs for others. Despite this circumstance, the relative income gap between the rich and the poor did not widen during the post-Eisenhower years: In effect, the government's programs exercised a leveling influence that enabled the income of Americans in the bottom-income quintiles to grow at least in

133

equal proportion with the advances that took place in the upper-income quintiles.

The policies of the post-Eisenhower years, "the failed policies of the past," provided unprecedented numbers of new jobs for Americans, raised the nation's real income at rates of growth favorable to those of the past, reduced poverty significantly, assured that Americans would not grow more widely separated in the proportions of income they received, and in these many ways helped the nation adjust to the challenge of the crowded generation. And all these results were achieved without the alleged wild or uncontrolled expansion of the public sector.

The nation passed through tortuous times in the post-Eisenhower years. Facing circumstances that befell no other major Western country, the government and the nation at large did not fail. The tradition of the government's intervening to protect people from powerful economic forces beyond their control—a tradition that began in the depression years and of which the nation is still proud—was no less evident in the post-Eisenhower years. But whereas during the 1930s the depression was a problem of obvious severity in almost everyone's eyes, the birth and divorce rates, combined with the changing role of women in the work force, and the subsequent burgeoning labor market that hit the nation's economy throughout the late 1960s and 1970s, were not. The difficult challenges facing the 1930s were broadly recognized at the time; those facing the 1960s and 1970s largely were not. In this difference lies the opposite political responses of the two eras: the new confidence in government that spilled out of the 1930s and lasted through the middle of the 1960s, with the Democratic liberal coalition its prime beneficiary; in contrast, the growing frustration with government that captured the public in the 1970s with the gathering conservative ranks its great beneficiary.

The failure to understand and appreciate the challenge confronting the post-Eisenhower years was indeed a boon to the conservative critics of government. For above all, it meant that critics could continue to flail away at the public policies of the post-Eisenhower years without ever having to face up themselves to the crucial economic issue of the times: how to address the onset of the crowded generation. From 1965 to 1980, unemployment had climbed only moderately. Even inflation, though higher than during the 1950s, always remained in single figures save only for the years of the stiff international oil price hikes.[25] As a result, the nation's personal income continued to rise at healthy rates of growth even after inflation. Exactly what alternative policies could the critics propose? What policy would meet the coming of the crowded generation and not in itself result in either a decidedly higher unemployment rate than that of 1965–80, a higher rate of inflation, or an increased number of public-sector jobs and the regulation of private-sector wages, precisely what the critics of strong government wanted to avoid? Realistically, could any alternative escape the consequences of the crowded generation? Those who toured the nation roundly upbraiding the "failed policies of the past" and advocating their overturn did not address this essential question. In point of fact, they were not asked to, and still they are not. The policies of the post-Eisenhower years ultimately became discredited not by reality but by a national debate that rarely, if ever, acknowledged the realities of those years.

# 5

## Public Opinion and the Public Programs of Government

AN EXAMINATION of the success or failure of governmental activism would be incomplete without a consideration of how the American people felt about the priorities and programs of government. From the late 1960s onward, the question was frequently raised as to whether Americans approved the spending of the ever-climbing amounts of money needed to deal with matters such as poverty and whether, during increasingly difficult economic times, the public supported extending the regulatory powers of government to deal with issues such as environmental pollution. A silent majority, it was claimed, held rather different views.

Few would deny that the government's poverty programs received widespread support at or near the start. Programs to help disadvantaged people here and abroad, Vista and the Peace Corps, were so popular at their inception that thousands of volunteers had to be

137

turned away. The first Gallup poll taken on people's general feelings about the poverty program came in early 1966, when the poverty program was still in its infancy. The Gallup organization asked the public: "Overall, do you have a favorable or unfavorable opinion of the antipoverty program nationwide?" Across the nation, 61 percent of those holding an opinion were favorable, 39 percent were unfavorable.[1] A majority of similar proportions, a landslide in terms of presidential elections, had elected Lyndon Johnson two years earlier. Equally important was the breadth of support for the programs. The antipoverty effort received a favorable plurality in the north, south, east, and west, in the business and professional worlds, in the white-collar and blue-collar worlds, in communities large and small.[2] An aide to President Nixon once advised him to ask: "How does it play in Peoria?" Apparently, back in early 1966, the government's antipoverty effort played fairly well there.

Nor was it only in general concept that the American public expressed its approval. The public reiterated this view on questions about many of the major individual components of the attack on poverty.[3] For example, as far back as 1960, five years before funding for the antipoverty effort began its dramatic expansion, Gallup polls revealed that the American public gave greater priority to enlarging funds for both slum clearance programs and medical programs for the elderly than it gave to balancing the federal budget by cutting government spending. With respect to job training, too, each year from 1961 through 1964, according to Gallup's findings, government programs to provide training and public-service jobs to unemployed youths were favored by greater than 70 percent of the public. Year after year, as well, the public supported the Medicare concept by more than a two-to-one majority.

The public's support did not soon erode. Even by the early 1970s, opinion polls indicate that the public's attitude about the effort to alleviate poverty had changed hardly at all. Louis Harris found substantially the same majority (56 percent to 28 percent) supporting the programs when his polling organization asked Americans in 1970 whether they agreed or disagreed with politicians who advocated an increase in federal programs to help the poor.[4] By 1972, funding for the antipoverty programs had grown significantly, and that year Harris asked the public in May and again in August if it supported increasing federal aid to the poor. The answer the public gave was again decisively in the affirmative, each time by majorities of almost two to one.[5] Gallup polls taken in 1972 show a similar result.[6] And once again, a plurality of the public was in favor of further expansion of the poverty programs in every region of the nation, in every size community, in every age group, in each income group, in all educational groups, and in every occupational group. By 1972, after the programs had already greatly expanded, each and every segment of the nation continued to support increasing federal aid to the poor.[7]

One possible counterargument is that by this time the public's support had settled mainly behind those programs oriented toward training people for jobs and finding them work rather than programs that provided food stamps, housing, and other subsidies. Public concern about welfare bums and chiselers had intensified and grown nasty. And it is true, in view of this, that the public overwhelmingly supported job training and work programs as ways to deal with poverty. Gallup had found toward the close of 1968 that almost 80 percent of the public favored programs that would guarantee enough work so that each person in the job market could earn $3,200 a year.[8]

Nevertheless, while less in agreement, the public remained persuaded that other forms of poverty assistance were also essential.[9] When Gallup asked the nation in 1969 whether the government should give food stamps to all families whose incomes were less than $3,100 a year (then approximately the poverty level), 60 percent of the public favored such a program, 31 percent opposed it. Gallup found that a clear majority also supported governmental assistance to improve the living conditions of the poor in the cities. In 1972 Gallup went further to ask whether or not the tax money then being spent on six antipoverty programs should be increased, reduced, or kept the same? More than 70 percent of the public wanted spending on each of the six antipoverty programs to be either increased or maintained at current levels. Indeed, comparing the segment of the public wanting to increase spending to that wishing to reduce or end spending, the public, by two-to-one margins, wanted to *increase* spending for five of the six programs: low-rent housing, rebuilding the inner cities, Medicaid, programs for the elderly (including social security), and improved education programs for children from low-income families (Table 4). For each of the six antipoverty programs, in fact, including outright welfare payments, an increase in spending rather than a decrease in, or end to, spending was favored by a larger proportion of the public.

As the 1960s ended, former Census Bureau Director Richard Scammon and his colleague Ben Wattenberg surveyed the findings of opinion polls to place the im-

*Table 4.* Attitudes of the American Public Toward Federal Spending on Six Social Programs, 1972 (in percent)

| | Increase spending | Maintain spending at present levels | Reduce spending | End spending |
|---|---|---|---|---|
| Low-rent public housing | 40 | 40 | 12 | 4 |
| Education for low-income children | 62 | 28 | 3 | 2 |
| Rebuild inner cities | 51 | 29 | 11 | 5 |
| Medicaid | 52 | 35 | 6 | 2 |
| Programs for the elderly | 74 | 21 | 2 | 0 |
| Welfare programs to help low-income families | 30 | 41 | 18 | 6 |

*Source:* William Watts and Lloyd A. Free, *State of the Nation* (New York: Universe Books, 1973), pp. 295–96.

portance attached by the public to the poverty issues in perspective. They wrote: "Some of these [priorities], such as Medicaid, poverty programs, aid to cities, are issues that five or ten or fifteen years ago would have been considered rather far out for middle-of-the-roaders. Today they are clearly in the mainstream."[10]

Even the main approaches chosen by the government to reduce poverty found far more popular support than did the major available alternative, a guaranteed income. Proposals to provide a guaranteed income were consistently opposed by popular majorities. From 1965 to 1976, for example, an average of all polls shows "that approximately 60 percent of Americans oppose a guaranteed income, 30 percent favor it, and 10 percent have no opinion."[11] In 1970, after a titanic struggle, the federal government rejected this choice, too.

Thus, public approval remained firm from the very inception of the poverty programs. As late as 1976, when funding reached its zenith relative to the GNP, the public was in no mood to turn the corner and reverse the programs. Although the percentage of Americans wanting reductions or outright termination of some programs stood at higher levels (almost 40 percent) in 1976 than in earlier years, the proportions of the nation that favored maintaining or increasing spending were: rebuilding the inner cities, 70 percent; programs to help the elderly, 95 percent; welfare programs to help low-income families, 61 percent; food stamps for low-income families, 60 percent, and programs to help the unemployed, 79 percent.[12] It is noteworthy that not even the principal conservative tome on welfare, authored in the 1970s, cited a single national poll reporting more than 50 percent of the American public to be specifically in favor of cutting back on programs for the poor.[13]

Despite the continued support of a clear majority of Americans, it cannot be denied that by the middle 1970s popular opposition to some of the programs had grown measurably. Equally important, the antipoverty issue was no longer among the public's top several priorities. As popular support narrowed, governmental action changed and greatly slowed. The last major new initiative the government undertook in the antipoverty arena came in 1973 with the establishment of the CETA program and public-service jobs for unemployed adults. Indeed, by 1976 the totality of the government's social programs, federal and state, peaked in expenditure relative to GNP. From 1960 through 1976 the proportion of the GNP of the social programs had grown every year from 5 percent to 11 percent.[14] But with the popular majority behind them no longer as overwhelming as in earlier years, the social programs were to grow no more after 1976. To the contrary, in the final three years of the 1970s, federal and state spending on social programs declined slightly, taking about 1 percent less of GNP than they had at their peak in 1976.[15]

Among the other great initiatives of the post-Eisenhower era, as described in previous chapters, are the programs to reduce environmental pollution. The series of environmental policies the federal government adopted, increasingly tough after 1968, accounted for the single greatest source of increase in the regulatory costs of government during the 1970s. By 1979, the administrative costs of pollution control were treble those of 1974. At the end of the 1970s, private industry alone was paying more than $10 billion each year to comply with the regulations.[16] A Business Roundtable survey of forty-eight major corporations found that more than 60 percent of the costs to these companies of new federal regulation in the 1970s stemmed from environmental controls.[17]

Virtually every American had direct experience with problems of air and water pollution. Most had seen "unexplained" haze hanging in the air, or smoke billowing out of huge stacks, or dead fish washed up onshore. Many knew someone whose wheezing was worsened by air pollution or had seen signs warning swimmers to stay away from foul water. By the 1960s, these experiences were familiar to people across America. Earlier tolerated as part and parcel of the effects of production, in the highly prosperous times of the post-Eisenhower era, degradation of the environment was increasingly viewed as impinging on the quality of life.

The Clean Air Act amendments, by which the federal government would impose and enforce air quality standards for the first time, were adopted in 1970. A Louis Harris poll of that year found that a phenomenal 83 percent of the public then agreed that more money should be spent on the control of air and water pollution.[18] When asked which of ten governmental programs should be cut the least, an absolute majority of the public (55 percent) identified the antipollution programs. Of the ten programs, the antipollution programs ranked first in importance after education (poverty ranked third). A minuscule 3 percent of the public felt that the antipollution programs should be the first to be cut.

Overwhelming popular favor for environmental controls continued in 1972, just as Congress was in the process of adopting far-reaching water-pollution-control legislation. In both May and August of that year Louis Harris found that more than 80 percent of the public favored spending more money to curb air and water pollution; only 10 percent were opposed.[19]

Unquestionably, public support for environmental controls remained substantial throughout the rest of the decade. For example, each year from 1973 through 1979 the Roper poll found that more than 60 percent of the public wanted the environmental programs either maintained or expanded. In no year during the 1970s did as much as 25 percent of the public feel that the environmental programs had gone too far.[20]

Americans divided not so much on the desire to clean up the environment or on the willingness to spend more money toward that goal but on, rather, exactly how the costs of the effort should be assessed. Whereas the public favored the expenditure of only modest amounts of tax money, a series of polls by Harris, Roper, and the National Opinion Research Corporation found that clean-up costs in the form of higher prices for products and services were acceptable. The public's willingness to pay higher prices continued undiminished even into the years of higher inflation, from 1974 onward, generally remaining true by majorities of more than two to one.[21] In point of fact, the programs have operated in precisely this manner. Less than one-quarter of the direct costs of the environmental programs are financed by the government through taxation; about three-quarters of the costs are borne directly by the private sector to meet the government's regulatory standards, costs that would eventually be passed on to the consumer as an element of the price structure.

Thus, the concept that a silent majority of the American people existed that disapproved the actions of government during the post-Eisenhower years fails to describe the facts in the cases of two pivotal priorities of government of those years, the reduction of poverty and the control of environmental pollution. On both of these issues, governmental activism was closely aligned with the views of the public. Whatever else may have been on the minds of Americans in the 1960s and 1970s, the reduction of poverty and control of pollution were unquestionably among the most important items Americans wanted resolved. Moreover, not only did large majorities of Americans desire governmental activism to tackle these two issues, but in each case they also favored the principal methods of attacking the problems that the government opted to use.

# 6

# The Present and the Past

WE DERIVE a final important measure—a test, if you will
—of the effectiveness of the policies under review by
making comparisons with the performance of the policies which followed them. The new social and economic policies, after all, were aimed at reversing the
problems allegedly caused by the policies of the past.
Yet these problems, I have argued, were far more apparent than real, and the performance of the policies of the
post-Eisenhower era was far better than had been understood. Having been founded on a series of misperceptions, the social and economic policies of the Reagan era have consistently, across numerous areas, fallen
short of the results achieved during the post-Eisenhower years.

Movement away from the policies of the post-Eisenhower era, beginning in the late 1970s,[1] accelerated
dramatically after Ronald Reagan's election to the presidency. In the first two years of the Reagan era alone,

tax rates were cut substantially on both business profits and the personal incomes of most Americans. Senator Robert Dole called it the "largest tax cut in U.S. history."[2] The government streamlined regulations across a whole series of industries, most notably in banking, oil, and transport. The social welfare programs also came onto the chopping block. Public service jobs under CETA were completely eliminated, future investment in public housing was nearly brought to a halt, and AFDC aid to working mothers was eliminated. Such spending, President Reagan said, was "a matchless boondoggle," part of a welfare system that had become "a faceless mass waiting for handouts."[3]

The objective was to reduce the government's intervention into people's economic lives. The policymakers believed this would result in increased incentives for both individuals and corporations to make greater contributions. Breathing more easily under less burdensome taxation and regulation, businesses would begin to invest more money and hire more employees. Individuals would work harder and longer hours earning higher after-tax wages. Rather than taking public money, welfare recipients would decide to take jobs if the rewards for productive work were made greater than welfare.

With all the new activity, the theory continued, the economy (and with it the government's own coffers) would flourish while unemployment (and with it poverty) would decline. Investment and productivity would grow along with the international competitiveness of our industries. The additional revenues raised from the resurgent economy coupled with cuts in the rampant waste of government would pay for the tax reductions and also permit an increase in spending on defense.

Nor was this all. Even as unemployment fell, so, too, would inflation. The reduced tax and regulatory burden of government coupled with a proper monetary policy and strong productivity gains would bring inflation down well beneath the double-digit heights they reached in 1980. Following the drop in inflation, interest rates would decline, leading to still more investment and production. A long, stable recovery would result. Having stamped out the fires of inflation, there would be no need for a renewed anti-inflationary policy that might cut the recovery short.

The economic policies of the 1980s were built on two main premises: first, that the economy had deteriorated in the generation prior to 1980; and, second, that the growing burden of governmental interference and mismanagement had been the principal cause of this deterioration. So it was with social policy, too. The percentage of Americans who were able to get out of poverty on their own had begun to decline after 1968, and the new holders of power believed that governmental policies had been a principal cause. They claimed that welfare policies had become so generous as to lead people to take public assistance instead of work. As a result, the numbers of Americans who were or would have been in poverty save for the government's assistance—known as "latent poverty"—rose during the 1970s. To stem the spread of latent poverty, the architects of the new policies proposed a straightforward solution. The economic advances of the new policies, coupled with the reduction of the disincentives of welfare to employment, would reverse the disturbing rise of latent poverty. By way of reduced governmental interference, then, the new policies proposed to turn around the twin problems that the old policies of the post-Eisenhower years had allegedly caused: the economy's decline and latent poverty's rise.

Of course, a complete change of policy did not come about in the Reagan era. Congress did not grant the president everything he requested. In 1981 his major budget and tax proposals were adopted nearly without change. But after 1981 Congress enacted tax increases to replace some of the revenues lost through the massive 1981 tax reduction; it also scaled down some of the administration's proposed domestic cuts; and it defeated some of the proposed outlays for defense.

Nevertheless, the alterations of policy after 1980 were substantial when compared with the then existing policies. Compared with the policies in place in 1980, the changes of policy after 1980 amounted by 1984–85 to an inflation-adjusted tax reduction of $93 billion a year (about 12 percent), a lowering of nondefense spending by $56 billion a year (10 percent), and an increase in defense spending by $36 billion a year (15 percent).[4]

In the four years alone from 1981 to 1985, the federal government's tax receipts declined from 20.1 percent to 18.6 percent of GNP. Marginal tax rates (taxes on the last dollar earned) fell by greater than 10 percent for Americans with the average family income and above.[5]

Taxes on business dropped by even more. As a proportion of profits, effective tax rates on corporations were sliced nearly in half, from above 30 percent to 15.8 percent, and indeed dropped to 12 percent for manufacturing firms.[6]

On the spending side, cuts in some social programs had already predated the Reagan administration. For example, total real spending on means-tested cash assistance programs (such as AFDC) had begun to decline as early as 1978, falling from $38 billion in 1977 to $32 billion in 1980 and then to $28.8 billion in 1984.[7] After 1980 the total real amount spent on all means-tested programs—combining both the cash and noncash benefits of food stamps, school lunches, public housing, and Medicaid—also started to decline.[8] So, too, did spending on employment and training programs, which fell from $13 billion to $4 billion from 1981 to 1986.[9]

If not a true revolution in policy, the program that came into place after 1980 had a distinctly different orientation to it than the one that had characterized most of the post-Eisenhower era. Apart from the reductions in virtually all personal and corporate taxes as well as in spending on programs for the poor, the administration claimed savings for businesses due to a series of eliminated or reduced regulations amounting to nearly $75 billion over five years.[10] Moreover, as we have seen, military spending had risen significantly. "It's time to try something different,"[11] President Reagan had said in early 1981. If he was not the victor on each and every detail, certainly the Congress had enacted the general thrust of the program put forth by President Reagan, the most vocal critic of the policies of the post-Eisenhower years.[12]

## The Results: Poverty in America

### General Trends

Sometime during the late 1970s, American policy toward the poor began to reverse itself. Not only had total real spending on means-tested cash assistance started falling during 1978, but after 1980 tighter restrictions were placed on eligibility to AFDC, food stamps, and unemployment benefits with the hope of limiting the alleged disincentives to work built into the welfare program. Much of this assistance had been considered by the new policymakers to be wasteful and even counterproductive. During those same years from 1978 to 1985, a net addition of 13 million new jobs came into being in the American economy, nearly 2 million new jobs a year. Real income per person rose by 12 percent. All the pieces were fitting into place, it would seem, to begin making inroads into poverty by means of the engine of private economic growth.

The opposite took place, however. Not only did the numbers of Americans in latent poverty grow by some 8 million people after 1979, a rate of increase double that during the decade before,[13] but, reversing the trend of prior years, the numbers of Americans actually living in poverty also grew (see Graph 1). The numbers living in poverty rose from 15 million in 1979 (6.8 percent) to

22 million in 1985 (9.1 percent), a rise of one-third.[14] The reference here is to net poverty, since it includes all Americans living in poverty even after public assistance of every kind is included. The period after 1979 constitutes the first sharp rise in net poverty in America for any extended period since prior to 1950.

*Graph 1.* Americans in Poverty, 1965–85
(in percent)

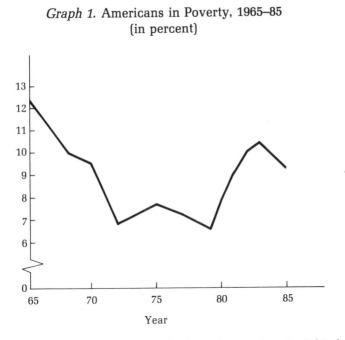

*Sources:* Charles Murray, *Losing Ground: American Social Policy, 1950–1980* (New York: Basic Books, 1984), p. 65, Figure 4.5.

Robert Greenstein and Keith McKeown, "Poverty Rises Faster When Non-Cash Benefits Counted," Center for Budget and Policy Priorities, Table 2.

Bureau of the Census, "Estimates of Poverty Including the Value of Non-Cash Benefits: 1979–1982."

American children fared badly as well. The proportion of children living in poverty, according to the standard Census Bureau definition, climbed from 16 percent to 21 percent, a rise of more than 3 million children.[15]

During this period, too, a remarkable shift occurred in the distribution of family income. After remaining nearly constant throughout most of the post-Eisenhower era, the after-tax income going to the top one-fifth of American families grew from 40.6 percent in 1980 to 42.3 percent in 1984, while that of every other income group declined.[16] Between 1980 and 1984 median real family income dropped by 8 percent (from $6,900 to $6,400) for the bottom one-fifth of American families on the income ladder, while rising by 9 percent (from $37,600 to $40,900) for the top one-fifth.[17]

As the income distribution shifted and governmental programs became more restrictive, other related developments took place. The numbers of low-income children of single working parents eligible for Medicaid fell by more than 500,000, while the numbers of families needing emergency food assistance rose.[18] The decline in infant mortality among blacks, which had been rapid since 1965, slowed sharply, by nearly half, after 1982.[19] Although it is hard to measure homelessness accurately nationwide, all acknowledge that the numbers of homeless not only increased, but now began to spread beyond single individuals to include families with children. Figures for New York City, for example, reveal that the numbers of homeless families with children grew fourfold from 1976 to 1984, from 633 to 2,354 families. They continued to climb to 4,365 families by early

1986, nearly seven times the numbers recorded a decade earlier.[20] According to the U.S. Conference of Mayors, the numbers of families needing assisted housing rose by 40 percent nationwide during the 1980s.[21] Estimates of the total numbers of homeless in America in 1986 ranged widely from a low of 300,000 to more than 2 million.

Homelessness is in many ways at the vortex of impoverishment. It combines the many horrors of poverty. A tenement is gutted by fire, or is gentrified, and the tenants lose their homes, the jobless among them unable to find other affordable homes in a tight housing market. Or a textile worker loses his job, eventually becoming unable to pay his rent. He is evicted and no longer has the up-front money (both first and last month's rent plus deposit) to get another. Having no place to wash, no place to sleep, and no place to get messages, homeless people find it ever more difficult to land a new job. Virtually all who live on the streets are unemployed. One homeless American observed: "Can't get no job without a home, and you can't get a home without a job. They take one and you lose both."[22] Homelessness becomes self-perpetuating.

Living on the streets with never more than a few hours' sleep, always keeping an eye out for the police, badly disorients people. About a third of the homeless are former patients of mental hospitals; of the remainder, many soon show signs of mental disorder. Likewise, being on the streets raises alcohol consumption, especially during the wintertime—a way of keeping warm on bitter cold nights—leading some who once were not abusers to become alcoholics. While a few have chosen to be on the streets, the large majority have not. For them, the pain and indignity of homelessness is indescribable.

Surely responsibility for the rapid spread of homelessness and hunger among families with children or the sharp slowing of the decline in infant mortality does not lie solely with the policies taken up during the past few years. It is just as certain, however, that those policies did not help matters, either.

Consider the impact of the new policies on low-income American families. Suppose that spending on the government's various assistance programs had been able to reach the same percentage of poor families with children in 1985 as in the late 1970s.[23] In 1979 the benefit programs lifted 38 percent of the poor families with children in America above the poverty level. By 1985 this figure had fallen to 24 percent. That is, by 1985 the cuts in funding for the assistance programs since 1979 had caused about 750,000 American families with children to fall beneath the poverty level. From 1981 onward nearly half the increase in poverty among families with children can be accounted for by the declining impact of the assistance programs in removing families from poverty.

In most of the years of the post-Eisenhower era, as Graph 1 shows, the percentage of Americans living in poverty declined. Why didn't this trend continue in the Reagan era as it had earlier? The answer lies partly in the faulty premises that led proponents of the new social policies to curtail public assistance. The policies of the Reagan era presumed that people lived off welfare instead of working, and that if people worked, they would lift themselves out of poverty. Neither of these presumptions is generally valid. First, the impact of welfare on the willingness of males in the labor force to work is not nearly as substantial as the proponents of the new policies suppose. Second, even if it were, the ability of poor Americans, male or female, to rise out of poverty through taking jobs in the private economy has been far more limited than the new policies comprehend.

### Welfare and Work

That welfare has had a generally minor impact on the behavior of males in the labor force is shown in many reputable studies of unemployment.[24] It is demonstrated, too, by a series of welfare experiments.[25] Most compellingly, however, the limited impact of welfare on unemployment is made clear even in the findings of the strongest critiques of the welfare system.

To demonstrate the corrosive effect of welfare on the incentive to work and earn one's way out of poverty, Charles Murray analyzed the labor-market behavior of American males from 1950 to 1980 in a detailed year-by-year manner. His highly publicized study, *Losing Ground*, uncovered what Murray considered to be conclusive evidence of the strongly negative influence of welfare on work.

Murray makes his much-cited case by showing how the expansion of welfare under the Great Society after 1965 led young black male adults to become unem-

157

ployed and to drop out of the labor force. In these respects, blacks aged 16–24 behaved differently from any other group of males. The unemployment rates of the young adult black males climbed quickly from 1965 to 1980. That their rates of joblessness rose at a markedly sharper pace after 1965 than did those of young adult white males, or indeed, those of black or white males beyond age 24, is shown on Table 5. In addition, young black male adults were virtually alone in dropping out of the labor force in large numbers after 1965. As Table 6 documents, only young black adults experienced this sharply negative trend in dropping out of the labor market. White young male adults had no such experience. Their dropout rates actually fell during the same period. Nor did the dropout rates of older blacks or older whites grow by much, as Table 6 also indicates. Murray's evidence and analysis thus document that welfare's expansion had a strong negative impact on young male black adults, distinguishing them from all other groups of males.

For the moment, grant the Murray case in full. Accept the validity of his argument that the Great Society's liberalization of public assistance caused unemployment and dropout rates to rise sharply among young black male adults, and that in this the young black male adults were largely unique. The fact is that these young black males comprise only one in eleven of all unemployed males in America (and a similar low percentage of the males who have dropped out of the labor force), the other ten in eleven coming from groups that Murray's own evidence shows as having behaved reason-

*Table 5.* Labor Force Experience of Six Selected Groups of Males: Unemployment Rates, 1965 and 1979

| | Blacks and Others | | | Whites | | |
|---|---|---|---|---|---|---|
| Age | 16–19 | 20–24 | 35–44 | 16–19 | 20–24 | 35–44 |
| 1965 | 23.1 | 9.3 | 5.1 | 12.8 | 5.9 | 2.3 |
| 1979 | 31.5 | 17.0 | 5.8 | 14.1 | 7.4 | 2.5 |
| Change | +8.4 | +7.7 | +0.7 | +1.3 | +1.5 | +0.2 |

*Source:* Calculated from Charles Murray, *Losing Ground: American Social Policy, 1950–80* (New York-Basic Books, 1984), p. 247, Table 7.

*Table 6.* Labor Force Experience of Six Selected Groups of Males: Withdrawal Rates, 1965 and 1979, in percent

| | Blacks and Others | | | Whites | | |
|---|---|---|---|---|---|---|
| Age | 16–19 | 20–24 | 35–44 | 16–19 | 20–24 | 35–44 |
| 1965 | 44.9 | 10.2 | 5.8 | 42.4 | 14.7 | 2.3 |
| 1979 | 52.1 | 19.9 | 9.1 | 32.7 | 12.4 | 3.6 |
| Change | +7.2 | +9.7 | +3.3 | −9.7 | −2.3 | +1.3 |

*Source:* Calculated from Charles Murray, *Losing Ground,* p. 248, Table 8.

ably responsibly.[26] Thus, even as Murray develops the detailed evidence to support his case in *Losing Ground,* his thesis unwittingly reaffirms the opposite conclusion that welfare's impact on unemployment and dropout rates among males has been marginal. As many other studies also demonstrate, the influence of welfare's expansion after 1965 has been no more than minor on the great majority of the unemployed males in America.[27]

Nevertheless, even if the impact of public assistance has been marginal on most groups of males, the fact that young black males behaved differently cannot be ignored. That they did so after 1965 is strongly suggested by the evidence of Tables 5 and 6. That evidence, however, does not show that the expansion of governmental assistance in and about 1965 forms the dividing line after which their behavior became unique. In fact, the rise in their withdrawal rates from the labor market did not originate in 1965. The trend had commenced well before that. According to Table 7, the withdrawal of young black males aged 16–19 from the labor market had been going on since the mid-1950s. The table shows that the pace of their withdrawal actually *slowed* after 1965 compared with the rise during the decade before, completely contrary to the Murray thesis. Only the 20–24-year-old black males, then, fit the thesis Murray puts forth. Young black males aged 20–24 constitute just one in twenty of the more than 4 million unemployed males in America. And even their declining rate of participation in the labor force resulted at least partly from the steeply climbing rate of school enrollment (a rise of 11 percent) after 1964 among black males aged 20–24.[28]

As even the Murray analysis confirms—let alone a multitude of other studies—the expansion of public assistance after 1965 had no more than a marginal impact on unemployment and labor force participation rates among males. To have cut public assistance programs

*Table 7.* Labor Force Withdrawal Rate Among Nonwhite
Males Aged 16–24, in percent

| Age | 16–17 | 18–19 | 20–24 |
|-----|-------|-------|-------|
| 1954 | 53.3 | 21.6 | 8.9 |
| 1965 | 61.7 | 33.3 | 10.2 |
| 1979 | 68.3 | 42.2 | 19.9 |
| Change 1954–65 | +8.4 | +11.7 | +1.3 |
| 1965–79 | +6.6 | +8.9 | +9.7 |

*Source:* Calculated from Charles Murray, *Losing Ground,* p. 248,
Table 8.

thinking that the programs were a primary cause of
unemployment was wrong. It focused attention on the
very few who became unemployed as a result of public
assistance, forcing cuts which hurt the large majority of
recipients of the programs. Simultaneously, the policy
of blaming public assistance missed—and was thereby
unable to do anything about—the most important problems facing people who live in poverty in America.

### The Jobs Picture

For those able to work—whether males or females—
a crucial element of the problem facing the poor has
been the inability of the economy to generate enough
full-time work for Americans at wages above the poverty line. The past two decades have been harsh ones
from the standpoint of American workers who were on
the bottom of the ladder. First came the entry of the

baby boomers into the labor market from 1964 to 1980 resulting in a chronic shortage of jobs. This despite the net addition of 28 million new jobs in those years, a performance that still fell short by 2 million of the net increase of 30 million Americans who entered the labor market. Nothing other than an increase in governmental assistance could bridge the gap.

This became evident even in the very early period from 1965 to 1970. The immediate response to the wave of baby boomers was not so much a job shortage as employment in part-time jobs. At the start the economy generated large numbers of such jobs with the surprising result that, initially, unemployment even among the first wave of baby boom adults *declined.* In 1965 fewer than half of the 16–19-year-olds who were employed worked in part-time jobs; from 1965 to 1970 about four out of five of the new jobs for this group were part-time.[29] From 1965 to 1970 the greatest rise took place in the proportion of the labor force working in part-time jobs of any five-year period from 1945 through 1980.

During the 1970s, however, most of the jobs generated in the economy, though leaving a shortage of about 2 million, were full-time jobs at levels of occupational status generally equivalent to those of the 1960s and 1950s.[30] Fewer than 20 percent of the jobs added between 1973 and 1979 paid less than the poverty level for a two-person family (about $7,500 a year in 1986 dollars).

After 1979 the situation worsened yet again. The period began with the added shortage of 2 million jobs that had accumulated over previous years. But the demographic picture appeared bright as the 1980s would no longer have to contend with the mounting numbers of baby boomers. The numbers entering the labor force began to taper off after 1979, by fully one-fifth compared with the ten years before 1979 (1.9 million new workers entered a year after 1979 versus 2.4 million earlier).[31] Unfortunately, this declining rate in the net addition of new workers was met by an equal decline in the generation of new jobs, leaving nearly the same shortage of jobs by the mid-1980s as had existed earlier.

Then, on top of the continuing job shortage, much of the newly created employment from 1979 onward came in the form of part-time and/or low-wage jobs. About 45 percent of the 9.3 million new jobs that came into being between 1979 and 1985—more than 4 million jobs—paid below $7,500 over a year.[32] Recall that less than 20 percent of the new jobs between 1973 and 1979 paid such low wage rates, fewer than half as many as in the years between 1979 and 1985. Nearly thirty percent fewer full-time jobs have come into being yearly following 1980 than occurred during the 1970s. That the employment situation grew significantly worse is revealed in the numbers of Americans working in part-time jobs because they were unable to find satisfactory full-time work. The numbers of such workers jumped from 4 million in 1980 to nearly 6 million in 1983, and remained at 5.3 million even in 1986, a rise of one-third over 1980.[33]

Neither in the post-Eisenhower nor in the Reagan era was poverty or joblessness the product of public assistance programs. To the degree that the programs secured proper funding, public assistance operated to lift Americans above the poverty level who had been—and still are—left stranded by the private economy's shortage of jobs paying above-poverty-level wages. The experience of the 1980s demonstrates, no differently from the post-Eisenhower years, that as long as substantial shortages of jobs at living wages continue to exist, only governmental activism can check and reverse the rise of poverty in America.

## The Results: The American Economy

Following 1982, two years into the Reagan era, America entered into one of its longest sustained peacetime recoveries of the twentieth century. In length, only the recovery of the 1960s clearly outlasted it. During one of the years—1984—the GNP rose by more than in any year since 1951. The economy added a staggering 4 million new jobs in that one year alone. Moreover, unlike during any other recovery, the fires of inflation did not begin to be rekindled, even when the recovery moved into its third and fourth years. At 4 percent in 1984 and 3.8 percent in 1985, the rate of inflation bested not only 1980 by a large margin (when it hit 13.5 percent), but also any of the seven years prior to that. Then, dropping below 2 percent in 1986, the rate of inflation for that year was the best in a generation. A decline in interest rates followed the decline in inflation: at 7.5 percent at the end of 1986, the prime rate was about one-third what it had been in January 1981. As all this happened, the stock market soared. America's economy certainly seemed far better off by the mid-1980s than it had been during the last listless decade of the post-Eisenhower era, the "soggy" 1970s.

Nevertheless, at the end of 1986 still more than 13 million Americans either had no job or were underemployed in part-time jobs, having been unable to find adequate full-time work. The unemployed and underemployed in 1986 numbered nearly 2 million more (a 1 percentage point increase) than in 1980 when the Carter administration left office. This despite the *reduced* numbers of new workers needing jobs as the baby boom's sweep into the labor market ended in 1979–80. The average length of an individual's unemployment rose from 10.8 weeks in 1979 and 11.9 weeks in 1980 to 15.6 weeks in 1986.[34]

How can this seeming contradiction be explained? Essentially by understanding that the economy of the 1980s was not moving forward in the manner that we have been asked to believe.

Surface images of both the 1980s and the 1970s aside, the nation's economic growth during the Reagan era— in most respects during even the *best* years of economic growth in the years after 1982—has not strengthened compared with the 1970s. To the contrary, as the following pages demonstrate, it has weakened. This result stands as evidence of both the economy's unrecognized power in the 1970s and the misconceived policies— based on many misunderstandings of the past—that the new holders of power enacted in the 1980s.

Nor is this all. The economic achievements that did occur during the Reagan era were purchased at an extraordinarily high price, one making America's future decisively less secure. Indeed, the achievements followed not from the supply-side economic theories that the critics of the post-Eisenhower era advanced; rather, they arose from practicing and ultimately abusing the Keynesian theories the critics had condemned. Moreover, the achievements themselves became possible mainly because of a welcome lessening in the 1980s of the twin burdens under which the economy of the 1970s continuously had to struggle—a thinning of the waves of baby boomers entering the labor force and a reversal of the skyrocketing international oil prices.

### Comparing the Record of the 1980s with That of the 1970s

By no means did it become "morning in America" during the years following 1980. Rather than quickening, the pace of economic growth during the Reagan era slowed noticeably when compared with the 1970s. True, during 1984 the United States had its single best year since 1951. Nevertheless, the picture for the entire period up through 1986 casts a very different shadow.[35] From 1980 through 1986 the GNP (2.5 percent average growth per year), industrial production (3.0 percent average growth per year), and per capita disposable income (1.8 percent average growth per year) all rose at real rates below those of the 1970s. From 1970 through 1980 the GNP grew on a yearly average of 3.2 percent, industrial production climbed by 3.8 percent, and per capita income grew on average by 2.0 percent a year.

Most of the factors that stand behind economic growth rose more slowly, too. The addition of 10 million new jobs from 1980 to 1986 (1.7 million per year on average) is heralded as a magnificent achievement of a reborn economy in the Reagan era—a testimony to the payoff of supply-side Reaganomics to American workers. Actually, it amounts to nearly 20 percent *fewer* than the 2.1 million new jobs added on average each year throughout the 1970s. Generating a high proportion of part-time jobs, the 1980s have created still fewer full-time jobs a year as compared to the 1970s.

Nor has investment as a percentage of GNP grown any stronger during the 1980s, not gross private investment, nonresidential investment, or investment in new plant and equipment. All have remained either the same as in the 1970s (gross private investment) or indeed diminished (nonresidential investment and investment in new plant and equipment). This despite the emphasis that the policies of the Reagan administration have placed on increasing investment.

Productivity rises in businesses across the whole economy have remained unchanged (1.1 percent rise per year from 1970 to 1980 and from 1980 to 1986). Only in the case of the productivity of our manufacturing businesses do we, at last, find rates of growth that have been stronger in the 1980s (3.4 percent per year) than in the 1970s (2.5 percent per year).

Critics of the economic policies and performance of the post-Eisenhower years have an answer to these many unflattering comparisons. They believe that the initial two years of the 1980s should, by right, be considered the legacy of the old policies. It is alleged that the recession of the early 1980s, the most severe since the depression, came about as a result of mounting pressures from many prior years of misguided govermental economic and social policies. A disputable claim, the severity of the recession of the early 1980s can equally be seen as resulting from the spiraling rise in the world price of energy that occurred from 1979 to 1981 coupled with the conflict between the new administration's highly expansionary fiscal policy on the one hand, and its highly restrictive monetary policy on the other.

Whatever is the case, it is possible to avoid the controversy to some degree by confining comparisons to the recovery years of the 1980s (1983 through 1986) and the last recovery years of the 1970s (1976 through 1978, ended in mid-1979 by the giant oil price rises that year). These comparisons show the same result as did the earlier ones. Far from being stronger, economic growth during the recovery years in the 1980s has generally been weaker than in the 1970s.[36]

For example, from 1983 through 1986 real GNP grew by 4.0 percent a year, nearly one-quarter below the 5.2 percent a year it had climbed during the last recovery of the 1970s. Industrial output expanded at 5.3 percent yearly from 1983 to 1986, only two-thirds the 8.5 percent yearly growth from 1976 through 1978. Adding 2.5 million jobs a year on average, the 1980s' recovery has fallen nearly 1 million jobs short of the 3.4 million yearly average from 1976 to 1978—a 25 percent drop. Real income per individual American, at a 2.7 percent annual growth rate from 1983 to 1986, rose somewhat less than the 2.9 percent annual growth from 1976 to 1978. Productivity of the nation's businesses grew at substantially the same annual rate (1.7 percent) in both periods, as did total private investment (about 16 percent of GNP).

Why has America's economic performance in the 1980s often fallen below the standards set in the post-Eisenhower era? Supply-side economics told us that business would begin to invest and to produce more, leading the way to economic recovery, when the dead weight of government was removed. All that held business and a recovery at bay was the heavy hand of big government. Government had to lower taxation and regulation.

This theory was far removed from the reality of the past, however. Taxation of business had already been on the decline for two decades prior to 1980. Also, investment had grown as a proportion of GNP in the 1970s, not diminished, when compared with earlier decades. The diagnosis of the past was all wrong.

As a result, so were the theory's projections for the future. Business investment in new plant and equipment had risen in real terms by an average of 6.5 percent yearly in the last half of the 1970s, 1976–80.[37] Then came the big tax cuts in 1981. When the president's tax plan was enacted, Donald Regan, then Secretary of the Treasury, predicted that business investment would rise by 11 percent annually after inflation for at least the first five years, 1981–86.[38] Instead, the reverse took place.

Following the tax cuts in 1981, business investment in new plant and equipment did not rise by even as much as the 6 percent a year on average it had done before 1981, let alone by the 11 percent a year that Secretary

Regan had projected. Investment instead declined in 1981, once again in 1982, and still again in 1983.[39] In fact, hard though it may be to believe, the fifty corporations that had the lowest tax rates under the new law (*minus* 8.4 percent on average) actually *reduced* their investment in new plant and equipment by 21 percent from 1981 through 1983 compared with the prior three years, even while raising their dividends to stockholders by 14 percent.[40] The fifty companies that paid the highest tax rates (averaging 33 percent) in 1981–83 enlarged their dividends by 11 percent as well, but also increased their investment by 4 percent. No relation whatsoever existed between the magnitude of the tax breaks and business investment. Consider the individual example of General Electric. From 1981 through 1983 General Electric made $6.5 billion in domestic profits. The company paid no income tax at all; it actually got nearly $300 million back in tax rebates from the government (a tax rate of minus 4 percent). In absolute terms it claimed the largest single tax benefit during those years. The company did raise its dividends to stockholders by 19 percent. All the same, it cut its investment in new plant and equipment by 15 percent.

Why did no connection exist between massive tax breaks and the business investment that was supposed to spur the recovery? Robert McIntyre and Dean Tipps point out, "In the real world, companies invest only when they need new plant and equipment to produce products they can sell to consumers. When consumers don't spend money, plants are idled and new investment drops. Corporate decisions are driven by demand side market forces rather than supply-side theories."[41] This is why investment fell after 1980, even during the first recovery year of 1983, and surged upward only after 1983, when the recovery was already well under way. The Reagan recovery was fueled not by increased investment and enhanced productivity, as supply-siders had predicted, but rather by a surge of demand-side growth (in line with the discredited Keynesian theory) arising from exaggerated increases in federal deficits and increased personal borrowing.[42]

In fact, even with the recovery, investment in new plant and equipment did not come close to equaling the performance of the 1970s. At about 5 percent a year, the rate of rise in such investment during the present recovery has been only three-quarters that of the final recovery of the 1970s.[43]

Wrong about the performance of the past, the theory underpinning the new economic policies proved unable to provide an effective blueprint for forward progress. Economic growth has been noticeably weaker in the 1980s than it had been during the 1970s. Nor has even this slowed economic growth spread out to the large majority of Americans. It has instead gone nearly exclusively to those in the top half of the income scale.

When William Jennings Bryan first described the theory of trickle-down economics, he said, "There are those who believe that, if you will only make the well-to-do prosperous, their prosperity will leak through on those below."[44] The Reagan era's supply-side economics promised great gains not just to a few, but to nearly all. It projected higher after-tax profits for business and, through new business investment and output as well as lower personal taxes, more jobs and higher after-tax income to labor. During a time of powerful economic growth, practically everyone would win. That appeal constituted a main source of the political and popular support behind Reaganomics. Based on a faulty reading of the past, however, the entire construct soon collapsed. Economic growth slowed. In the end the system disintegrated into little more than a form of trickle-down economics whose weakened trickle failed to reach very far down the income ladder.

The single area of decisive improvement—although even it is more apparent than real—has been the rate of inflation. The critics of the post-Eisenhower policies had claimed that inflation climbed in the 1960–80 years because of increases in governmental expenditures coupled with the method of paying for those expenditures—the growth of both the budgetary deficits and the money supply. Reversing this process, it was thought, would slice inflation. Clearly the 1980s show otherwise.

Budget-cutting rhetoric aside, the Reagan era did not produce—nor did the president propose—an overall cut in federal expenditures. Instead, owing largely to soaring defense expenditures, federal government expenditures as a percentage of the GNP rose from 1980 to 1986. The budget deficits also mushroomed, tripling in size. And, after 1982, the money supply grew at its fastest pace since 1950. Nevertheless, even in spite of this triple threat, inflation *fell* dramatically, and it stayed at a low level as the recovery continued. It did so because the causes of the rise in prices in the post-Eisenhower era mainly lay elsewhere than in the theories of governmental profligacy and mismanagement that the critics had alleged.

As much as anywhere else the causes lay in the spiraling oil price rises from 1972 to 1980.[45] In those eight years energy prices never rose in any single year by less than 6 percent. They climbed by about 50 percent in 1973–75 and then again in 1979–80. The 1980s provide a striking contrast. Energy prices increased by a tiny 1.2 percent in 1982, actually fell in 1983, stayed constant in 1984, and rose by less than 2 percent in 1985. They then plunged by one-fifth in 1986.

It is no surprise that inflation never flamed as the recovery of the 1980s lengthened. Instead of rising by an average 7.5 percent annually in the recovery years of 1976 through 1978 and then by 37 percent in 1979, the price of energy stayed essentially constant from 1983 to 1985 and then fell significantly in 1986. This primarily exogenous development certainly helped to steady prices in the 1980s. A lowering of import prices into the United States as a result of the sharp 40 percent rise of the world price of the dollar from 1981 to 1985 also contributed to the low rate of inflation.

The impact of the rising dollar on inflation after 1980 was substantial both because it reduced the prices of imports and because it acted to restrain the wage demands of American workers whose industries, because of the rising dollar, became increasingly vulnerable to imports. According to one analysis, reduced energy price rises after 1980 coupled with the soaring dollar had, by 1983, caused the rate of inflation to be 2.9 percent lower than it otherwise would have been.[46] The noted analyst Allen Sinai, chief economist of Shearson-Lehman Brothers, found that by the following year, 1984, the rising price of the dollar had produced a cumulative effect since 1980 equal to a 5 percent annual reduction of the inflation rate.[47] If the dollar had remained constant in price from 1980 through 1984, inflation would have been 5 percentage points higher in 1984. Were this to have happened, the rate of inflation for 1984 (at 9 percent) would have equaled the inflation rate during 1978, the third year of the last recovery of the 1970s.

The fall in the inflation rate in the 1980s has not come primarily from any fundamental strengthening of the American economy. Inflation has declined because of both the elimination of the international energy price increases, against which the economy of the 1970s forever had to struggle, and the rising price of the dollar (about which more later). Were it not for these factors, the rise in prices in the 1980s would have been substantially the same as in the 1970s.

During the Reagan era, no improvement has taken place in the fundamentals of the American economy. As often as not, the growth of total output, industrial production, real income, jobs, and investment failed to reach the rates of the 1970s. In fact, the levels of growth of the American economy from 1980 to 1988 are likely to be the slowest for any eight-year period since the depression. Even inflation's decline is deceptive, for a simultaneous reversal of the same two factors that caused its decline in the 1980s (the fall in world oil prices and the rise of the world price of the dollar) could easily rekindle inflation in future years.

The slimmer rates of real growth generated in the 1980s as compared with the 1970s do have an effect. Because of them, America will have to sustain continued economic advance (with rates of growth obtaining in 1985 and 1986) through to the end of 1992 in order to accumulate the same real growth of GNP (32 percent) that occurred from 1970 to 1980. This growth through 1992 would have to take place with no interruption, without any recession. Were such a feat to occur, the real growth in GNP during the twelve-year period from 1980 through 1992 would then simply equal the growth achieved during the ten years of the so-called "soggy" 1970s.

## The Costs of the New Economic Policies

Apart from the question of growth, the policies that the misunderstandings of the past set into motion have carried with them a series of other costs that Americans will bear for many years. The unnecessarily large tax cuts of the Reagan era coupled with the spending increases helped generate federal budgetary deficits that had risen at one point (1983) by $140 billion a year, nearly tripling those the Reagan era had inherited. By 1985–86 the budget deficits still ran more than $120 billion higher than in 1981. At least $70 billion of the increased deficit resulted from the decline in revenues forthcoming from the various tax changes that occurred after 1980.[48] Additional contributions to the deficit came from increases in defense spending and spending to finance the deficit, the combination of which outpaced declines in nondefense spending by about $20 billion.[49]

The deficit began to climb immediately after the new budget's enactment. Starting at 2.7 percent of GNP in 1981, the deficit had grown to 6.2 percent in 1983 and remained at around 5.0 percent in 1985 and 1986, all record peacetime deficits.[50]

The rise that took place in the size of the total federal debt compared with the size of the economy shows poignantly the difference between the policies of the 1980s and those that dominated the post-Eisenhower years. Ever since World War II the total federal debt as a proportion of GNP had remained steady or declined. From 1970 onward it had stayed relatively constant, within 33 to 38 percent of GNP.[51] The final budget under the Carter presidency ended in a total federal debt of $1 trillion, or 33 percent of the GNP of $3 trillion for that year. Ten years earlier the total federal debt had amounted to $372 billion, or 37 percent of the GNP, which was then $1 trillion.

This picture changed dramatically following the budget alterations of 1981. Immediately, in 1982, the government's total debt as a proportion of GNP began to shoot upward. By 1984 it had hit 40 percent of GNP; the federal debt had touched and passed 50 percent of GNP by 1986. It had climbed by 17 percent in five short years after having remained virtually unchanged for more than a decade prior to 1981.

The skyrocketing deficits came about largely because both the view of the past and the ensuing economic theories upon which the new policies were based were in error. Much of the increased size of the deficits grew out of the massive tax reductions, implemented because taxes were thought to have stifled the economy. Yet taxes had not risen in the post-Eisenhower years in the manner that had been claimed, neither on individuals nor on businesses.[52] Nor did taxes have the relationship to production and growth that supply-siders had theorized from their faulty understanding of past history. Consequently, neither investment nor production rose to anything like the levels needed to replenish the revenues forgone from the tax cuts. To the contrary, since business investment and total output generally slowed in the Reagan era, deficits soared as the result.

In theory, the deficits could be counterbalanced to some degree by reducing the wasteful spending of government. According to conventional wisdom, waste had become rife in government after many years of excessive liberal spending. Many—not just the president—argued that cutting waste could bring the deficits down.

This, again, reflected a serious misunderstanding of the past, as the Reagan administration soon learned. At the end of 1981, the new administration represented as one of its major cost-saving achievements the discovery that 8,500 dead people were still being sent social security benefits. Correcting that wasteful spending produced a savings of about one-fiftieth of 1 percent of social security payments, something worth carrying out but hardly a solution to the mushrooming federal deficits. In total, the president's commission on inefficiency in government uncovered far less waste in domestic programs (below $5 billion) than was needed to produce a significant dent in the deficit.[53] To cut more, and thus to go beyond the commission's findings, would constitute substantive policy changes and cuts in real services, not elimination of waste, as history subsequently proved.[54]

With the vastly enlarged deficits that resulted from these misunderstandings have come a whole series of disturbing consequences. First, the mounting interest charges on the enlarged debt consumed an additional 6 percent of federal budget revenues by 1986, thereby reducing the amount that could be spent for productive purposes, whether it be for education, environmental improvements, social programs, or defense. By 1986 paying off just the interest on the debt took up 17 percent of federal revenues, 6 percent more than the 11 percent in 1981.[55] Six percent of the federal budget is meaningful. It is sufficient to pay the bills for nearly every penny of the increased federal spending that took place on all programs for the poor during the post-Eisenhower era.

The situation might be less severe had the increased borrowing, which limits our ability to spend in the future, been utilized in ways that would improve our economy's strength and growth in the future. Yet we have already seen that the tax cuts did not lead to higher levels of private investment; nor has public investment in either education or the economy's infrastructure grown. In fact, spending on education has declined in the Reagan era from 7.4 percent to 6.9 percent of GNP.[56] The borrowing, instead, has been used chiefly to finance the current private consumption of taxpayers, the takeover of companies by one another, and defense spending. By borrowing for spending today at the price of both narrowing future choices and building a stronger economy for tomorrow, the policies of the Reagan era have brought America toward darker rather than brighter horizons.

Nor does this represent the greatest of the costs. The swift collapse of America's manufacturing trade in world markets, despite the increases in manufacturing productivity, also grew out of the new policies. In brief, the new policies led the real rate of interest to climb sharply in the United States, which helped spur a rise in the world price of the dollar, placing America's manufacturing industries at a severe disadvantage in world markets.

When the government borrows more (as long as others do not borrow less) *and* the growth of the supply of money has simultaneously been restricted, the interest rate must go up. It cannot be otherwise. When federal borrowing rose to record heights in 1982, the government was simultaneously following a policy—as it had been doing for three years—of restricting increases in the money supply. This policy, by necessity, produced a rise in the real rate of interest (the difference between the nominal interest rate and the rate of inflation). In fact, in 1982 the real interest rate climbed to a historic record and remained at historically high levels thereafter. From 1982 through 1985, despite the sharp declines in the nominal interest rate, the real interest rate remained three to five points higher than it ever had been in the post-Eisenhower era, or at any time since World War II.[57]

The dollar became more attractive with higher real interest rates, so that the rise in real interest rates in the United States laid the foundation for a sustained and dramatic strengthening of the dollar in world markets. The dollar rose by around 35 percent in price relative to the currencies of our trading partners, and 45 percent relative to the currencies of the other OECD nations.[58]

In turn, the rising dollar led imports to become cheaper.* It equally caused our exports to become more expensive. The combination, in turn, undermined the international trade of our manufacturing industries.

The rising budgetary deficits had a truly disastrous effect on the foreign trade of America's manufacturing industries.[59] Prior to the Reagan era, American manufacturing had held its own in world markets. Our worldwide balance of manufacturing exports and imports generally remained positive, as Graph 2 shows. It did so throughout most of the 1970s up through 1981. Thereafter, as the dollar continued to climb in price, our manufacturing imports grew like wildfire and our exports remained stagnant. Whereas in 1981 our trade balance was a positive $12 billion, by 1985 it had plummeted to a negative $102 billion, a staggering change of $114 billion in a mere four years (see Table 8). As a

---

*Thereby dampening inflation rates, which demonstrates—notwithstanding the conventional wisdom—how a rise in federal budgetary deficits can work to lower inflation.

Graph 2. United States Balance of Trade in Manufactures, 1970–85 (in billions of dollars)

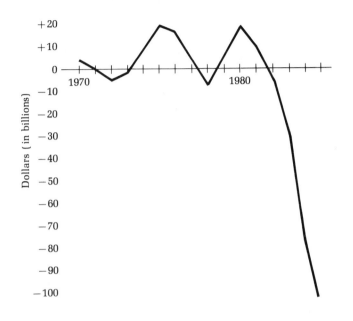

Source: *Economic Report of the President,* 1987 (Washington, D.C.: U.S. Government Printing Office, 1987), p. 362, Table B-102.

result of this turnaround, more than 2 million jobs at decent wages either were destroyed or failed to materialize, helping to explain why the economy generated far fewer new full-time jobs a year in the 1980s than it did in the 1970s.

Reversing itself, the dollar began to fall sharply in 1985–86 with the result that the trade deficit has possi-

*Table 8.* Manufactured Exports and Imports, 1981–85
(in Billions of Dollars)

|      | *Exports* | *Imports* | *Balance* |
|------|-----------|-----------|-----------|
| 1981 | 154,283   | 142,475   | +11,808   |
| 1982 | 139,716   | 144,022   | −4,306    |
| 1983 | 132,409   | 163,449   | −31,040   |
| 1984 | 143,142   | 221,515   | −78,371   |
| 1985 | 145,383   | 256,984   | −101,601  |

*Source:* President of the United States, *Economic Report of the President, 1987,* p. 362, Table B-102.

bly hit bottom. Yet, given the hazards of reestablishing customers once they have been lost, it will likely be sometime before our manufacturing industries are able to make substantial inroads into the negative trade balance.

Another development also followed in the process. In a few short years, the United States was transformed from the largest creditor nation in the world to the leading debtor nation in the world, thereby becoming ever more dependent on the goodwill of foreign countries to sustain its economic growth. "We now know the miracle of supply side economics," said C. Fred Bergsten, director of the Institute for International Economics, in 1986. "The miracle is that foreigners supply a large part of the goods and foreigners supply most of the money. Without the huge influx of capital from around the world, the U.S. recovery of the last 3 or 4 years simply could not have occurred."[60]

## The Reckoning

Perceptions do matter, for in American politics perceptions constitute a foundation for belief and action. "Reagan's success as President has accomplished what his ideas have not," William Schneider of the American Enterprise Institute observes. "If Reagan's conservative policies are working—and most people still think they are—then they must be right for our time. By demonstrating that his ideas work, Reagan has won many people to his cause who do not agree with his ideas or values."[61]

Yet to contemplate the wreckage of the Reagan era—the historic burden of debt that this very brief period placed on the next, the deep erosion of America's worldwide manufacturing position, the spread of both poverty and homelessness, and the slower growth in total jobs, in full-time jobs and decently paid jobs, in GNP, in income per American after inflation, and in investment for the future—leaves the mind spinning. The picture would be more dismal still (albeit perhaps better recognized) if the economy of the Reagan era had had to grapple with the onrushing numbers of baby boomers needing jobs and the spiraling increases in world energy prices that continuously faced the economy of the post-Eisenhower years.

Our undervaluing of the record of the post-Eisenhower years allowed the new policies to become the law of the land. Similarly, our mistaken perceptions of the present permit those policies to continue. To many the economy appears to have improved. No other view would be reasonable in light of the faulty perceptions most Americans have of the hapless failure of the government and economy in the decade that preceded the Reagan years. Only when compared with those mistaken images of failure can the record of the Reagan years possibly be considered a success.

Not only that. To rub salt in the wounds of the past, the very factors that helped lead Americans to underrate the nation's performance in the post-Eisenhower years—the surplus of labor and rise in international oil prices that unmercifully hit the 1970s—now, in their absence, prompt the reverse. The resulting massive decline in inflation and small decline in unemployment lead Americans to conclude that America's performance has improved when, in most respects, it has grown worse.

Of course, not everyone applauds the Reagan era. And one need not turn to liberal antagonists of the new policies to find stinging criticisms. President Reagan's own chief advisers, officials who held high seats of power in the administration when the policies were proposed and enacted, have some interesting comments of their own. People like Murray Weidenbaum, the former chairman of the President's Council of Economic Advisors, asserts: "We are basically a strong and wealthy country that is not managing its economic affairs too well. We are consuming more than we are producing. We are spending more than we are earning. We are borrowing more than we are saving. . . . This is not a period that will go down in the economic history books. . . ."[62] David Stockman, the president's former director of the Office of Management and Budget, is more blunt still. After pointing out that the fortieth president alone doubled the federal debt built up under the previous thirty-nine presidents all together, he says: "Historians will undoubtedly find these elephantine figures baffling. With the benefit of hindsight, they will know the immense damage to the nation's balance sheet and living standard that resulted from these . . . years of fiscal profligacy. By then, the secret of the Reagan era's fabulous free lunch will be beyond dispute."[63]

# Epilogue: Looking Back to the Future

In order to learn how America can move forward, we have looked backward to see where the nation has been. Dazed and dispirited, Americans entered the 1980s disturbed by the sensation that the prior twenty years had been largely misspent, that during all those years, bit by bit, we had traveled down the wrong road. The record of those years in the domestic spheres indicates otherwise. It reveals an era of constructive actions by both the government and the private economy to meet awesome challenges that only our nation faced. For nearly a decade, a spell of antigovernment rhetoric has taken hold. Evolving from a myriad of misunderstandings of the past, the spell has beckoned us to reject the twenty years of the post-Eisenhower era and the accomplishments that we as a nation, through government, achieved in those years. Only if we recognize the negative spell that has been cast can we draw renewed confidence from the knowledge that in the past we accomplished much through governmental activism to improve Americans' lives. Only then can we realize our capacity as a nation to do so again in the future. To continue to hold a falsely diminished view of the past, and to compare what the nation does today with that diminished view, is dangerous. It causes us to elect our leaders and to construct our policies on faulty premises. As important, it prompts us to ask less of ourselves as a nation—and thereby to advance less—even while we imagine that we are asking and advancing more.

## The Helping Society

The post-Eisenhower era began in 1960 with an optimism based on the desire of Americans to help each other. While believing deeply in individualism and self-reliance, Americans have historically also believed in giving and accepting help. Virtually every American receives help. Few of us make it entirely on our own without help (whether deserved or not) from parents, family, friends, or strangers. Many people acknowledge the assistance they have received on the path toward success. As Alexis de Tocqueville discovered, the concept of the American as a person who receives help and who also helps others in need was, even at our beginnings, as deeply rooted in the American psyche as the concept of the self-reliant individual who makes it on his own.[1]

The idea of helping others so characterizes Americans that America is, in many ways, a helping society. Nowhere does this crucial dimension of the nation demonstrate itself better than in the extensive voluntary activities of the American people. Each Thanksgiving and Christmas witnesses an outpouring of organized efforts across the entire nation to provide meals, presents, and comfort to families in need. In fact, these activities reveal merely the tip of the ongoing, everyday voluntary efforts of Americans. More than 40,000 nonprofit charitable groups exist in America, providing social services alone.[2] Apart from the many volunteers who freely give these organizations their time and skills, the number of paid employees—at nearly 700,-000[3]—amounts to more people than work in America's coal and steel industries combined. Together, the 40,000 social service organizations spend about $13 billion a year, of which $6 billion comes from private sources.[4]

Although fundamentally a helping society, America has, for many good reasons, simultaneously established a free market economic system. This kind of system calls for material rewards to be distributed unevenly and for those rewards to be an outgrowth of tough competition leading, hopefully, to hierarchies of achievement. That we continue to embrace such a system is a conscious and voluntary act on our part. The kind of economic system we have could be otherwise; we choose that it not be.

A direct implication of the kind of system we have accepted is that material rewards in the form of income will be distributed unevenly. At present, the top 5 percent of the income earners in the country receive about 20 percent of the pretax income, or quadruple the amount that an even distribution would accord them.[5] A foreseeable consequence of this highly uneven distribution of income is that some Americans who are relatively uncompetitive will be able to earn less, indeed sometimes so little that without other sources of income they will have to live in conditions the culture considers to be degrading and possibly even destructive. Consider, for example, the flip side of the quadruple share of the median income that the top 5 percent receive. This is the approximate amount received by the bottom 5 percent of American households. One-quarter of the present median family income comes to an average of less than $7,000 a year per household. This amount that the bottom part receives is $4,000, or 35 percent, beneath the poverty level for a family of four. It is beneath the poverty level even for a family of two.

In a free market economy, a variety of factors may make people uncompetitive or less competitive in the marketplace. Some of these factors can be influenced by the individual; but others may be beyond the individual's control. Individuals may be elderly or physically or mentally infirm; they may run up against racism or sexism; they may have such low intelligence as to be barely able to read; they may face a labor market gorged with an oversupply of workers so large that existing profit-making activities cannot absorb all of them; or they may be children. At least some of these Americans who are uncompetitive for reasons largely beyond their own control will be left in a condition of impoverishment. This is a foreseeable consequence of the competitive free market system.

How many Americans are there whose private income leave them in poverty for reasons largely beyond their control? No overall figure exists, partly because the definition of who fits into the concept of the "deserving" poor finds little agreement. Whatever definition one uses, however, the number of Americans who fit into it will be large. For example, there exist about 12 million elderly Americans over 65 years of age whose private sources of income leave them in poverty.[6] There exist more than 2 million disabled or ill Americans. And there are 16 million children. *Each* of these 30 million people is poor, or would be save for the government's assistance. No more than a minority of them have the power to change their situation by very much.

Also, an additional 20 million American adults aged 16–65 have levels of intelligence that are sufficiently low as to have made it an enormous struggle for them to learn how to read, let alone to graduate from high school. In this category, not all are poor by any means. Some have very good incomes. All the same, the kinds of jobs that have kept people of low intelligence out of poverty have been disappearing over the years even as the wave of young adult workers looking for jobs has swollen since 1965. With many fewer full-time jobs created during the past six years and some of these at very low wages, and with unemployment generally on the rise over the past twenty years, clearly not all in this group can lift themselves out of poverty on their own earnings. A growing number cannot. In this regard, females and minorities of both sexes who have low intelligence and no high school education, particularly those who came of age during the labor surplus years after 1965, would be especially vulnerable.

## The Alternatives

What, then, should America do? The only remedy that can succeed requires the intervention of a strongly activist government. Theoretically, of course, we have other options, including the option not to care about eliminating or even substantially alleviating poverty. "Let individuals fend for themselves, and let the chips fall where they may" is one response. To take this view as a nation, however, ignores the obligation we have to ease the consequences arising out of the choice we have made favoring a competitive market system (the consequence that numerous fellow citizens, for reasons largely beyond their power to change, will be left in conditions the culture considers degrading or destructive).[7] As important, this view stands outside the American character. It contravenes our history as a nation which cares for and helps people who are in distress.

It is also possible to care—indeed, to care deeply—but to decide that no active effort is needed on our part to eliminate poverty. Through growth and expansion, it is argued, the private economy will eventually end poverty. Yet this view fails on several grounds. The very problem of poverty, that some people will be left for reasons beyond their control in conditions the culture considers degrading or destructive, is inherent in the highly unequal distribution of material rewards that occurs in a competitive free market economy. To expect the same system whose own natural processes produce the problem also to solve that problem defies logic. It also defies the empirical evidence of the last twenty-five years which shows that, notwithstanding reasonably powerful economic growth, the reduction of poverty in America has occurred because of governmental assistance far more than the working of the private economy. Even were the private economy able to ameliorate poverty, it would take many years to do so.[8] The question then arises as to what to do in the meanwhile. Private, voluntary action is another possibility. This alternative has some decided advantages. It recognizes that positive action is necessary to resolve the problem of poverty; and it builds upon efforts that are freely given by individuals rather than imposed on individuals by government. Nevertheless, this choice—if viewed as the primary means of action—has one overriding weakness. That weakness is the insufficiency of private, voluntary activity when measured against the size of the problem.

Consider, for instance, the prodigious effort and publicity given over many months to "Hands Across America" in the attempt—one joined by hundreds of thousands of Americans—to help the homeless and the hungry in America. By raising the consciousness of Americans about the existence and degree of severity of the problems facing low-income Americans, "Hands Across America" provided an indispensable service. It also raised more than $50 million that has been utilized for a series of projects, such as the building of shelters, in a number of cities and towns.

However, even assuming that all of the $50 million reached the intended homeless and hungry beneficiaries in America (in actuality, about half of the $50 million went toward publicity and administration), the amount raised in this titanic private effort is relatively small compared with the need. All together, it totals the funds necessary for less than two days' expenditures of just a single governmental program such as food stamps. Food stamps serves about 22 million Americans, of whom the large majority have incomes below the poverty level, and the incomes of most of the remainder are nearly at the poverty level. The problem of poverty is indeed enormous.

Suppose there were an equally successful "Hands Across America" each and every day of the year, day in and day out. Suppose, further, that each and every penny collected was used for the poor with no administrative or publicity expenses. Even were this to happen, the total raised over an entire year ($18 billion) would amount to about one-quarter of federal income, food, and housing assistance to low-income persons in America. In actuality, the 40,000 charitable social service organizations in 1980 raised considerably less than $18 billion from private sources. Although they spent $13 billion, $7 billion came from the federal government itself; around $6 billion came from the voluntary contributions of private foundations and agencies, businesses, and individuals.

Voluntary activity is obviously an important ingredient, but it falls far short of meeting the problem in and of itself. In fact, were private efforts somehow to double so as to increase by $6 billion, it would constitute a mere one-third of the $20 billion of real cutbacks in federal governmental spending on social welfare as a proportion of the GNP that have taken place since 1980. Just as the growth of the private economy has been unable to compensate for governmental cutbacks let alone bring about progress in reducing poverty significantly, neither have private voluntary efforts been able to substitute for reduced governmental spending to ease the pain of poverty.

## Welfare: Guidelines for the Future

While only powerful governmental activism can address poverty effectively, Americans continue to struggle with unresolved conflicts about the role that government should play in eradicating poverty. On the one hand, serious doubts exist about the effects of the government's assistance programs on the incentive to work and the willingness to earn one's way out of poverty. Despite the evidence that can be produced suggesting otherwise,[9] these doubts persist. At the same time, Americans are troubled by and want to do something about the continued presence of poverty among millions of fellow citizens in this otherwise abundant land.[10] These conflicting concerns have gnawed at us for many years. They have rendered the governmental actions taken thus far incapable of succeeding in the public mind.

If the attempt to combat poverty in America is to succeed, these underlying conflicts must be resolved. To do so, governmental assistance programs will need to follow three guidelines.[11] First, to remedy the consequences of the competitive market economy outlined earlier, public assistance should raise all low-income persons who are in poverty for reasons beyond their control to a level of material condition that the society considers to be minimally dignified and safe. If we use the poverty line to define that minimum level, public assistance should bring all persons now living in poverty (persons who can reasonably be considered to have little alternative than to be in poverty) up to the poverty line or above.[12] It should do so both in the areas of income, inclusive of food stamps, and access to competent medical care. At present, the programs of most of the states fall far below this guideline.[13] Second, public assistance should be based on reciprocity. Persons who receive assistance should be required to make a reasonable effort, to the degree that they are able, to provide for themselves. This can be accomplished through the implementation of "workfare" programs.[14] Third, to retain the incentive system of a competitive free market, public assistance must leave intact the relative order of income and earnings received from the private economy. Using income and earnings from the private sector as a starting point, public assistance should never operate so as to raise one person above the privately earned income of someone else. Otherwise, individual incentives could be eliminated and the injustice inflicted that some people would end up with more from the community than other people derived from their own efforts.

These three guidelines call for major changes in the nation's public assistance programs, as is illustrated by the following example. Consider the head of a family of three who is out of work and has no income; a second such family head who works full-time earning the minimum wage ($7,000 yearly, still beneath the poverty line for a family of three); a third who earns $8,500, just about at the poverty line; and a fourth who earns $12,-000, or about $3,500 above the poverty line for a family of three.

A program calling for households with no income to be pulled up to the poverty line in return for reciprocity—that is, in return for active participation in workfare—would require a grant of nearly $8,500 plus medical benefits from the program to the first household. However, such public assistance would then put this household ahead of the privately earned income of the second family and equal to that of the third family, giving the heads of these two families little incentive to continue to work in the private economy. The program would thus need to assist these families, as well. Many different methods could be used to determine the amount of assistance granted. Assistance might be based, for example, on the median income, operating so as to bring every family up one-third of the distance between their own private income and the median. Using this method (and a median income of $25,000 for families of three), the first household would receive a grant of income of $8,333 (one-third of $25,000). The second household would receive a grant of $6,000 (which is one-third the difference between their income of $7,000 and the median of $25,000), resulting in a total income for the family of $13,000 ($7,000 plus $6,000). The third household would receive $5,500, leading to a total income of $14,000 for the family. Such incomes would then place these families above the fourth household, whose income from private sources was $12,000. This would be remedied by assistance of $4,333 to that family (one-third the difference between $12,000 and $25,000), resulting in a total income of $16,333 for the fourth family. A program based on this idea could be carried out simply for the majority of households through the usual tax process.

Such a program would achieve three vital goals. It would result in the virtual eradication of poverty in America; it would simultaneously require work or work-related activities from all individuals and families participating in the program; and it would eliminate the poverty trap whereby some people can get as much or nearly as much income by taking public assistance as they can earn by taking a job and working. It would thus deal directly with the major unresolved conflict that exists today in America between the desire to eradicate poverty and the concern that the attempt by government to do so will undermine or reduce the incentive to work.

However, the same proposal also raises very serious questions of its own. Among the most crucial of these questions concerns the cost. Can the nation afford such a program?

It is likely, of course, that the workfare program will itself raise the private income of participants to some degree through the successful placement of participants in private sector jobs (or, if participants previously had jobs, in better-paying jobs than they had before). Workfare programs now operate in experimental form in one or more cities in about two-thirds of the states. The programs differ widely, involving a mix of possible activities such as job search assistance to help participants locate private sector employment, job training and retraining, and compulsory community work. Even under mandatory workfare programs in which all welfare recipients must sign up for workfare, some people are usually excused, such as the infirm, or single parents with children under age 3. The experience of workfare programs indicates that they do bring financial benefits to both participants and the community. It equally indicates that far more money than is currently being spent will be needed to bring impoverished Americans —even those on workfare—above the poverty level. This is to say that, contrary to popular impression, workfare by itself cannot lift most impoverished Americans above the poverty level.

One constraint on the operation of the workfare programs has been the undersupply of jobs at above-poverty-level wages. Workfare cannot produce the desired result—to lift people out of poverty—without the availability of such jobs. Consequently, workfare has been able to make only modest gains for participants as compared with people who are on simple welfare. Workfare has moved participants into employment in the private economy at an average rate no more than one-tenth greater than for welfare recipients who are not in workfare programs.

The San Diego program is instructive.[15] In San Diego workfare is mandatory. The program involves a compulsory job search workshop and compulsory community work for thirteen weeks. Employment among workfare participants in San Diego grew from 35.5 percent to 41.9 percent over the first eighteen months, a rise of 6.4 percent; employment in a similar welfare group kept outside the workfare system in San Diego (a control group) rose by 5 percent during the same time, from 33.1 percent to 38.1 percent. Sixty-one percent of the workfare participants became employed at least sometime during the eighteen months compared with 55 percent of the control group. The average earnings of the workfare participants compared with the control group rose by $375 a year, or about 20 percent more than the earnings of the group outside workfare. Findings suggest that most other workfare experiments have had effects broadly similar to those of the San Diego program[16]—in fact, effects that are not much at variance with the results of the job training programs begun during the New Frontier and the Great Society years.[17]

Perhaps the most notable exception is New Hampshire, where the workfare program led to a reduction by 30 percent in the number of people on welfare from 1983 to 1986.[18] This important success, however, also corresponds with the job picture in the state. At just over 2 percent, New Hampshire's rate of unemployment stands at one-third the national average.

For a moment, let us return to the San Diego example. There the increase of $375 a year in earnings for workfare participants compared with the group outside of workfare brought the total earnings to an average of $3,700 per year for each workfare participant, still less than half of the poverty level for an urban family of three persons. Here again San Diego's experience was similar to that of most other workfare programs. In order to bring the workfare family in San Diego up just to the poverty line, additional direct public assistance beyond income from workfare would be required amounting on average to nearly $4,500 over a year to workfare families. This comes to about $1,000 more in assistance than the average participant in San Diego was in fact receiving (including the value of both AFDC and food stamps).[19]

The additional cost of bringing the income of workfare participants up to the poverty line, moreover, does not include the cost attached to the requirement that the relative order of income received from the private economy be maintained intact, which would necessitate granting assistance to persons above the poverty line but beneath the median income. Nor does it include the additional cost of administration, job search assistance, expanded job training and retraining efforts, and child day care involved in operating most workfare programs.

It doesn't include, either, the expenditure required to expand public assistance to embrace all the impoverished: for example, the cost of providing assistance to those many households in poverty headed by males or females who are now employed but are not at present covered by public assistance in most states; it does not include the expenditure necessary to provide adequate medical coverage to all low-income families (some of which are excluded from Medicaid by various regulations in the individual states); and it does not cover the cost for medical assistance to those families near to yet nevertheless somewhat above the poverty level, or to all other families who, presently, are made to become paupers before becoming eligible to receive long-term medical and nursing-home assistance under Medicaid. Finally, it does not cover the costs of enlarging social service programs that can help prevent the present problems in the future. For example, programs for youth known to have positive effects on participants' future education, skills, and employment are Head Start and the Job Corps. Neither of these programs is presently able to serve more than a small minority of the potentially eligible clientele. If expanded, the costs borne today for both programs would bring greater savings tomorrow. The same can also be said for other governmental programs. The special nutritional assistance given to low-income infants and small children, the WIC program, is an example.[20]

To carry out an effective reform of public assistance will thus be expensive when all these costs are added. The cost could mount up to $40 billion more, possibly even $50 billion, than is currently being expended. This in an era when gargantuan budget deficits would appear to make any new spending unthinkable. Yet the advantages of reform—that it would nearly eradicate poverty in the United States and do so in a manner as to give the public confidence that the incentive to work has not been undermined—are also large.

Part of the cost can be offset by implementing a national system to ensure that single-parent families receive the child-support payments from the absent parent. This action could generate up to $3 billion annually, although it, like the assistance system itself, will require a strongly activist governmental posture to be carried out effectively.

Still, even the strongest possible such action would offset only a fraction of the costs of reform. At a time of apparently severe fiscal constraints, can the nation afford to increase expenditure on public assistance significantly? The size of the deficit deeply influences views on proposals for policy change. According to House Majority Leader Thomas Foley (D–Wash.), "The pressure of the deficit is forcing Congress to think about [lesser] alternatives in a far more serious way than we otherwise would have done."[21] Considering the burden of the present deficits, it would seem immediately obvious that the nation could not afford to spend more money to combat poverty.

As have so many answers during the past handful of years, however, this answer follows primarily from our misunderstanding of the years between 1960 and 1980. Under the presumption that personal income and corporate profits taxes had risen from 1960 to 1980, the government from 1980 to 1986 gave up about $80 billion of revenues a year by reducing these taxes. The reality from 1960 to 1980 was otherwise, however. Contrary to the conventional wisdom, personal income and corporate profits taxes did not rise during the post-Eisenhower years. In 1980 they yielded in combination virtually the same amount (as a proportion of the GNP) as had been the case in 1960 or in 1955. As a result, personal income and corporate profits taxes in 1985 came to $80 billion less as a proportion of the GNP of that year than did those taxes in 1960 or 1955.[22] Were we simply to restore our willingness to pay personal income and corporate profits taxes at the level we paid in 1960 or 1955, not only would we solve the problem of how to fund public assistance, but we would simultaneously be able to reduce the deficit.*

Nor is it beyond mention that defense spending grew substantially between 1980 and 1986, rising by nearly $100 billion a year in real terms. A diminution of this giant increase by a mere one-third would provide the majority of the funding required for public assistance reform. Eliminating the continued eligibility of upper-income Americans for tax breaks that are not essential (for vacation homes, child day-care expenditures, and the like) would release several billion dollars more. Whether through a willingness to tax ourselves at the level we did under the presidency of Dwight Eisenhower, or a willingness to shift our priorities relatively marginally, the resources exist to reform public assistance successfully and indeed to act on other matters (including reducing the deficit) as well.[23]

---

*True, social insurance taxes rose on low- and moderate-income families between 1960 and 1980. At the same time, increased social insurance benefits to the elderly in the forms of both income and medical care, some of which would certainly otherwise have been shouldered by those families, partly offset the increased taxes. The remainder of the increased financial burden on those families could easily be offset now by adopting a lower social security tax and extending the lower tax to cover earned income above $45,000.

# Appendix

*Pollution Control: The Need for Governmental Involvement*

Just as in the effort to attack poverty, the government followed a policy involving strong intervention in its actions to regulate and control environmental pollution. Was any other course of action available that would have required less governmental interference? Could substantially similar environmental objectives have been met without the exercise of broad governmental power?

The necessity for a powerful governmental presence in the environmental realm is underscored even by many of the major critics of the government's policies. Milton Friedman, perhaps the most notable free-market economist of our time, emphasizes this point: "The preservation of the environment and the avoidance of undue pollution are real problems and they are problems concerning which the government has an important role."[1] Most pollution questions, according to Friedman, cannot be handled adequately by the free market alone. They can be successfully spoken to only by some form of governmental involvement. In the area of pollution, as in so many other areas, neither the costs and benefits nor the people affected can be satisfactorily identified,[2] with the result that no free-market mechanism exists to assure that the benefits of pollution control are received by those who bear the costs. Since no market mechanism exists, Friedman tells us, some mechanism must be invented. This is where the government enters.

Opponents of the government's current regulatory approach feel that it has led to a maze of standards and a cumbersome mass of rules. In the absence of a market to set an appropriate price for the privilege of polluting, they propose, as a substitute, that the government create such a price. The government could set a price by taxing pollution (some call such a tax "effluent charges"). After deciding how much pollution is tolerable, the government would place a sufficient tax (or charge or price) on various forms of pollution (from, say, an industrial plant or a car) so that the cost to the firm or the individual to pollute beyond the tolerable level would be more than the cost of the equipment to reduce pollution. Almost all the present regulations could be jettisoned under this approach. Firms and individuals would decide for themselves whether or not to pollute, and how much to pollute, depending upon the costs involved in reducing pollution relative to the taxation charges for producing pollution. If the tax was set properly, firms and individuals would find it cost effective to pollute only to the levels that the public, through its government, had determined to be tolerable. The role of government would be to decide tolerable pollution levels; establish pollution taxes, so as to do the most cost-effective job; monitor pollution to enforce the new taxation system; and determine how to employ any new revenues resulting from the taxes.

Possibly this approach would operate more efficiently than the current approach. Some evidence suggests as much, at least in some circumstances.[3] But few are certain. Some argue that pollution taxes may be virtually unenforceable as of now. They contend that the measurement of pollution emissions, upon which to assess the tax, is not sufficiently developed.[4] Even if such techniques were available, the staffing requirements needed to make measurements to enforce the tax would call for no fewer personnel than the current policy requires, and perhaps more.[5] There are others, too, who find that the figures offered by proponents of effluent charges sometimes amount to twice and even three times the actual cost of pollution control equipment. For automobile purchasers alone this could add up to an additional $1 billion to $2 billion annually.[6] The inherent difficulties in a pollution taxation system have led even some proponents of this system to conclude that the current regulatory and alternative taxation approaches must be further evaluated before firm conclusions can be reached.[7]

What is clear, however, is that the alternative proposed by these critics, including many renowned conservative economists, would require a high degree of governmental intervention in determining the desirable pollution levels, in setting pollution taxes, and in monitoring the taxation system. The government would likely be no less intricately involved nor exercise any less power or authority than it currently does. The issue is thus not how powerful the government should be or how much intervention it should undertake but rather how its intervention can be made more effective. Even on this score, the evidence is by no means clear that the taxation alternative would be more effective than the current approach.

# Notes

### 1 The Decline of Confidence in Government

1. The rise of antigovernment sentiment in America from 1960 to 1980 is documented in Seymour Martin Lipset and William Schneider, *The Confidence Gap: Business, Labor, and Government in the Public Mind* (New York: Free Press, 1983), pp. 13–29 and 33.

2. Ronald Reagan, "Inaugural Address," in Ellis Sandoz and Cecil V. Crabb, Jr., eds., *A Tide of Discontent* (Washington, D.C.: Congressional Quarterly Press, 1981), p. 212.

3. See William Watts and Lloyd A. Free, *The State of the Nation, III* (Lexington, Mass.: Lexington Books, 1978), pp. 215–16, and Lee Sigelman and David Lowery, "Party Identification and Public Spending Priorities in the American Electorate," *Political Studies* (June 1982), p. 227, Table 2.

4. *Los Angeles Times,* February 8, 1987; *Arizona Daily Star,* February 8, 1987.

5. *Arizona Daily Star,* September 5, 1982.

6. For example, apart from social insurance, the government's spending on social programs, as a percentage of both the federal budget and the GNP, reached its zenith in 1976, declining thereafter to the end of the decade; in 1978 reforms

to reduce regulation began in earnest with the deregulation of the airline industry; in 1978, again, policies designed to stimulate investment gained momentum with a substantial reduction in the capital gains tax; and, in the fall of 1979 and the early spring of 1980, projections for defense spending started to increase dramatically and monetary policy was made more restrictive. All these shifts of policy foreshadowed the policies to come. Because many of the policies emphasized after the 1980 election were in various stages of progress beforehand, I place the end of the post-Eisenhower decades at the end of the 1970s rather than at the end of 1980.

7. For two of the most recent examples of public opinion polls showing solid majorities of the public favoring these positions (polls by Yankelovich and Roper), see *Time*, March 30, 1987, p. 37, and *The Washington Post National Weekly Edition,* June 7, 1987, p. 38.

8. This paragraph is based on Ronald Reagan with Richard G. Hubler, *Where's the Rest of Me?* (New York: Duell, Sloan, and Pearce, 1965), pp. 40–41 and 52–54; Lou Cannon, *Reagan* (New York: Putnam, 1982), pp. 31–32, and Garry Wills, *Reagan's America: Innocents at Home* (Garden City, N.Y.: Doubleday, 1987), pp. 215, 222.

9. For Walter Payton's background, see *Chicago Tribune,* October 8, 1984.

10. Ronald Reagan, "Remarks at the National Italian-American Foundation Dinner," September 15, 1984, in General Services Administration, *Weekly Compilation of Presidential Documents,* Administration of Ronald Reagan, July 2–September 24, 1984, p. 1302.

11. Joseph M. Giordano, "Facts for the President's Fable," *Los Angeles Times,* September 18, 1984.

12. Ibid.

13. Lipset and Schneider, *The Confidence Gap,* pp. 22 (Figure 1–2) and 25 (Figure 1–3).

14. By representation, I refer to "substantive representation," in which, according to Hanna Fenichel Pitkin, *The Con-*

*cept of Representation* (Berkeley: University of California Press, 1967), pp. 209–40, "the people of a nation are present in the actions of its government" (p. 235). The government can take the lead or it can follow, but there must in the end be some correspondence between the public view and the actions of government.

15. Charles Murray, *Losing Ground: American Social Policy, 1950–1980* (New York: Basic Books, 1984).

16. Department of Labor, Bureau of Labor Statistics, *Handbook of Labor Statistics,* June 1985, p. 14, Table 4.

## 2 Politics and Performance from 1960 to 1980

1. Public-opinion figures in this paragraph for 1980 come from Warren E. Miller and the National Election Studies, *American National Election Study, 1980* (Ann Arbor, Mich., 1982), vol. 1, pp. 220–21; figures prior to 1980 are from Warren E. Miller et al., *American National Election Studies Data Sourcebook, 1952–1978* (Cambridge, Mass.: Harvard University Press, 1980), pp. 256–59. For further discussion of the change in public opinion about the government, see Chapter 4, note 1.

2. For example, see William Simon, *A Time for Truth* (New York: McGraw-Hill, 1978); George Gilder, *Wealth and Poverty* (New York: Basic Books, 1981); Milton Friedman and Rose Friedman, *Free to Choose* (New York: Avon Books, 1979); Gottfried Haberler, "The Present Economic Malaise," in William Fellner, ed., *Contemporary Economic Problems, 1979* (Washington, D.C.: American Enterprise Institute, 1979), pp. 261–90; E. S. Savas, *Privatising the Public Sector* (Chatham, N.J.: Chatham House, 1982); Jude Wanniski, *The Way the World Works: How Economies Fail—and Succeed* (New York: Basic Books, 1978); Ronald Reagan, "Inaugural Address," in Ellis Sandoz and Cecil V. Crabb, Jr., eds., *A Tide of Discontent* (Washington, D.C.: Congressional Quarterly Press, 1981), pp. 211–16.

3. Even many liberals became highly critical of the govern-

ment's programs, as is documented in Peter Steinfels, *The Neoconservatives: The Men Who Are Changing America's Politics* (New York: Simon & Schuster, 1979); Russell G. Fryer, *Recent Conservative Political Thought: American Perspectives* (Washington, D.C.: University Press of America, 1979), esp. Chapter 8; Lewis A. Coser and Irving Howe, eds., *The New Conservatives* (New York: Quadrangle, 1974).

4. Michael Harrington, *The Other America: Poverty in the United States* (Baltimore, Md.: Penguin, 1963), p. 128.

5. The quote is from ibid, p. 31; the introductory line is adapted from ibid.

6. Personal interview.

7. Poverty is conventionally defined according to level of income. The standard definition of poverty in 1959 was an income of $2,973 or less for a family of four in an urban area ($1,952 for a family of two). The levels are adjusted yearly so as to account for inflation. By 1970 the poverty income level was $3,970 or less for an urban family of four ($2,604 for a family of two). In 1979, the poverty level was placed at an income of $7,412 or less for an urban family of four ($4,878 for a two-person family).

8. The percentage of Americans in poverty in 1959 and 1960, using census figures, is in U.S. Bureau of the Census, *Statistical Abstract of the United States: 1979* (Washington, D.C.: U.S. Government Printing Office, 1979), p. 462, Table 758; hereafter cited as Bureau of the Census, *SAUS.*

9. Calculated from Bureau of the Census, *SAUS: 1980,* p. 469, Table 781. Figures on the number of dependents are in Sar A. Levitan, *Programs in Aid of the Poor for the 1980s* (Baltimore, Md.: Johns Hopkins University Press, 1980), p. 11.

10. Documentation of the public's attitudes is found in Chapter 5.

11. According to the Institute for Research on Poverty, when in-kind transfers from governmental programs are included, persons in poverty amounted to 4.1 percent of the population in 1980. (*Focus* 4, no. 3 [Spring 1981], p. 16). Other

estimates of the figure during the 1970s range from 4 percent to around 8 percent. See U.S. Bureau of the Census figures reported in "Redefining Poverty: Some Interesting But Loaded Choices," *New York Times,* April 18, 1982, section 4; Morton Paglin, *Poverty and Transfers In-Kind* (Palo Alto, Calif.: Hoover Institution, 1980), p. 61; Martin Anderson, *Welfare* (Stanford, Calif.: Stanford University Press, 1978), pp. 22–23; Sheldon Danziger, "The War on Poverty Revisited,' *Wharton Magazine* (Fall 1979), p. 63; Robert Haveman, "Poverty, Income Distribution, and Social Policy: The Last Decade and the Next," *Public Policy* (Winter 1977), p. 20; Robert D. Plotnick and Felicity Skidmore, *Progress Against Poverty* (New York: Academic Press, 1975), p. 85.

12. Anderson, *Welfare,* p. 26.

13. Ibid.

14. For per capita real disposable income 1950–72, see Bureau of the Census, *SAUS: 1975,* p. 383, Table 620; for the gross national product, see Bureau of the Census, *SAUS: 1975,* p. 381, Table 616. Here and elsewhere in the book, unless otherwise noted, yearly averages given for a period of years have been calculated on the basis of simple, not compound, rates.

15. Cited from data in the Survey of Economic Opportunity and Current Population Survey tapes reported in Plotnick and Skidmore, *Progress Against Poverty,* p. 112.

16. Sources are those in note 11.

17. A fuller description of the dynamics of change in the American labor force over the post-Eisenhower years is presented in Chapter 4.

18. The figures on absolute poverty in the remainder of the paragraph are from Plotnick and Skidmore, *Progress Against Poverty,* p. 114, Table 5.2, column on absolute poverty.

19. Ibid.

20. Ibid.

21. In fact, this group experienced only a 4 percent decline (from 65 percent to 61 percent) in the rate of poverty over the

entire 1959–70 supergrowth period. For families headed by females under the age of 25 in 1959 and 1970 who were living in poverty, see Bureau of the Census, *SAUS: 1972,* p. 332, Table 543; the total number of families headed by females under the age of 25 for 1970 is found in Bureau of the Census, *SAUS: 1971,* p. 39, Table 48, and for 1959 in Bureau of the Census, *SAUS: 1960,* p. 43, Table 44.

22. From 1965 to 1972, economic growth reduced poverty among nonwhite families headed by males under the age of 65 from 29.5 percent to 17.3 percent, and among white families headed by males under the age of 65 from 8.5 percent to 6.8 percent. For figures on absolute poverty, see Plotnick and Skidmore, *Progress Against Poverty,* p. 114, Table 5.2.

23. Sheldon Danziger et al., "How Income Transfer Programs Affect Work, Savings, and the Income Distribution: A Critical Review,' *Journal of Economic Literature* (September 1981), p. 996, Table 7. See also Chapter 6, pp. 157–161.

24. For the the increase in unemployment, see Chapter 4, Table 3.

25. Bureau of the Census, *SAUS: 1980,* p. 358, Table 577.

26. Ibid.

27. Sar A. Levitan et al., *Work and Welfare Go Together* (Baltimore: Johns Hopkins University Press, 1972), p. 52, Table 5.

28. A prominent criticism of AFDC lies in the unintended negative consequences that it may produce. Of particular concern is the possibility that AFDC may lead to the dissolution of families because often only families without fathers are eligible for AFDC support. To the degree this is so, however, alternative guaranteed-income programs to families provide no substitute. Experimental guaranteed-income programs have been associated with very high rates of marriage breakup. The results are summarized in Anderson, *Welfare,* p. 149.

29. Katherine Dickinson, "Transfer Income," in James M. Morgan et al., *Five Thousand American Families—Patterns*

*of Economic Progress* (Ann Arbor: Survey Research Center, University of Michigan, 1974), vol. 1, pp. 263–64.

30. For the number of recipient families and number of children in these families, see Bureau of the Census, *SAUS: 1980,* p. 358, Table 577.

31. Levitan, *Programs in Aid of the Poor,* pp. 34–35; Bureau of the Census, *SAUS: 1980,* p. 358, Table 577.

32. Dickinson, "Transfer Income," p. 272. This conclusion is confirmed by Lee Rainwater of Harvard and Martin Rein of MIT, who reanalyzed the data on the 5,000 families from 1968 and thereafter. See U.S. Congress, *Congressional Record,* 97th Cong., 1st sess., September 14, 1981, p. H6188.

33. The heads of almost 50 percent of such families worked in 1979, compared with the heads of 59 percent of such families in the early 1960s. For 1979, see Bureau of the Census, *SAUS: 1981,* p. 450, Table 754; for the early 1960s (1963) see *SAUS: 1965,* p. 344, Table 473.

34. See Chapter 6, pp. 157–161.

35. U.S. Senate, 96th Cong., Subcommittee on Nutrition, Committee on Agriculture, Nutrition, and Forestry, "Hunger in America: Ten Years Later" (Washington, D.C.: U.S. Government Printing Office, 1979), p. 43.

36. The few studies available suggest that food stamps have had mixed results concerning the alteration of usual nutritional levels for the average individual, in contrast to the findings of the Field Foundation on the change in the incidence of flagrant malnutrition. Yet, the same evidence finds that food stamps are more cost effective than guaranteed income as a method to treat malnutrition, although direct transfers of food are even more cost effective. See Maurice MacDonald, *Food Stamps and Income* (New York: Academic Press, 1977), pp. 64–76.

37. U.S. Senate, "Hunger in America," p. 11.

38. Danziger, "The War on Poverty Revisited," p. 62.

39. U.S. Senate, "Hunger in America,' pp. 16 and 41.

40. Ronald Andersen et al., *Two Decades of Health Ser-*

*vices: Social Survey Trends in Use and Expenditures* (Cambridge, Mass.: Ballinger, 1976), pp. 8, 20.

41. Ibid, p. 20.

42. Ibid.

43. By 1970, 65 percent of low-income people had seen a physician during the preceding year compared with 71 percent of high-income persons. The figures for 1963 were 56 percent and 71 percent,respectively. Andersen et al., *Two Decades of Health Services*, p. 44.

44. The mean number of prenatal visits to physicians among low-income people grew from 6.5 in 1963 to 9.6 in 1970. Andersen et al., *Two Decades of Health Services*, p. 58.

45. Ibid., p. 48.

46. For additional evidence supporting the same conclusion, see Lee Benham and Alexandra Benham, "Utilization of Physician Services Across Income Groups, 1963–1970," in Ronald Andersen et al., eds., *Equity in Health Services: Empirical Analyses in Social Policy*, p. 101.

47. Theodore Marmor and Andrew Dunham, "Federal Policy and Health: Recent Trends and Differing Perspectives," in Theodore Lowi, ed., *Nationalizing Government: Public Policies in America* (Beverly Hills, Calif.: Sage, 1978), p. 271.

48. Bureau of the Census, *SAUS: 1978*, p. 74, Table 106. The table also covers the white infant mortality rate.

49. One example: Infant mortality on seven Indian reservations in Montana declined from 31.5 per 1,000 to 16.6 per 1,000 just three years after the introduction of a supplemental nutritional program for pregnant women and children. Another example: The introduction of the food-stamp program and a comprehensive health clinic in Beaufort County, S.C., reduced the infant mortality rate from 62.4 per 1,000 to less than 17 per 1,000. U.S. Senate, "Hunger in America," pp. 46, 51.

50. The thirteen nations similar to the United States for which infant mortality rates were available both in 1965 and 1975—Austria, Belgium, Canada, China (Taiwan), Czechoslovakia, France, West Germany, Ireland, Israel, Japan, New

Zealand, the Soviet Union, and the United Kingdom—are found in Bureau of the Census, *SAUS: 1966,* pp. 901–2, Table 1288, and *SAUS: 1977,* p. 895, Table 1509. The infant mortality rates of the thirteen nations were between 19.5 and 29.5 per 1,000 births in 1965 (the figure for the United States was at the midpoint, 24.7 per 1,000).

51. Comparative figures on health expenditures are found in John G. Cullis and Peter A. West, *The Economics of Health* (New York: New York University Press, 1979), p. 17. At 0.2 percent a year after 1960, the yearly increase in health expenditures as a percentage of GNP in the United States was 0.04 percent above the average for the growth rates recorded in the other Western countries following 1960.

52. For 1940–70 figures, see Bruce Headey, *Housing Policy in the Developed Economy* (London: Croom Helm, 1978), p. 180, Table 7.2. For 1976 figures, see Bureau of the Census, *Social Indicators III* (Washington, D.C.: U.S. Government Printing Office, 1980), p. 154, Table 3/20.

53. For 1940–50 figures, see Headey, *Housing Policy in the Developed Economy,* p. 182; the figures for physically inadequate housing in 1960, 1970, and 1976 are based on Bureau of the Census, *Social Indicators III,* Table 3/6, p. 144. Because these latter figures are in the form of total number of households rather than percentages, I have recomputed the figures into percentages.

54. Levitan et al., *Work and Welfare Go Together,* p. 52, Table 5.

55. The results covering the history of employment before and after participation in CETA are from Laura L. Morlock et al., "Long-term Follow-Up of Public Service Employment Participants: The Baltimore SMSA Experience During the 1970s" (Baltimore: Johns Hopkins Health Services Research and Development Center, 1981), p. 44, Table 11; p. 33, Table 7.

56. The results covering the history of wages and earnings before and after participation in CETA are from ibid., p. 55, Table 14.

57. William Mirengoff and Lester Rindler, *C.E.T.A.: Manpower Programs Under Local Control* (Washington, D.C.: National Academy of Sciences, 1978), p. 14.

58. James L. Sundquist, *Politics and Policy: The Eisenhower, Kennedy, and Johnson Years* (Washington, D.C.: Brookings, 1968), p. 91.

59. Ibid.

60. These studies examined MDTA programs from 1963 to 1972, the year preceding the incorporation of the programs into CETA. For a summary of their results, see Jon H. Goldstein, *The Effectiveness of Manpower Training Programs: A Review of Research on the Impact on the Poor*, U.S. Cong., Joint Economic Committee (Washington, D.C.: U.S. Government Printing Office, 1972), pp. 2–3, 29–41. The results are also reviewed, with generally similar conclusions, in Charles R. Perry, "Manpower Development and Training Act," in Charles R. Perry et al., *The Impact of Government Manpower Programs* (Philadelphia: Wharton School, 1975), pp. 157–180, and Steve L. Barsby, *Cost-Benefit Analysis and Manpower Programs* (Lexington, Mass.: Heath, 1972). In estimating benefits, studies of manpower programs must make assumptions about how long the effects (or service life) of the programs can be expected to last. Perry (p. 158) finds that if one assumes only half the service life normally assumed, the benefits arising from the MDTA on-the-job training programs would still decisively outweigh the programs' costs, whereas the case for the MDTA in-house or institutional programs would then become questionable.

61. Garth L. Mangum and R. Thayne Robson, *Metropolitan Impact of Manpower Programs: A Four-City Comparison* (Salt Lake City, Utah: Olympus, 1973), p. 292.

62. Perry, "Manpower Development and Training Act," p. 158.

63. Irving Lazar, *Summary: The Persistence of Preschool Effects*, Community Services Laboratory, New York State University College of Human Ecology at Cornell University,

October 1977. For an annotated bibliographic summary of the many Head Start studies, see Ada Jo Mann, *A Review of Head Start Research Since 1969* (Washington, D.C.: George Washington University, 1978).

64. Bill Keller, "Sacred Cows," *Congressional Quarterly Weekly Report,* July 18, 1981, p. 1279. A multiplicity of other studies also generally show positive results. See Mann, *A Review of Head Start Research Since 1969.*

65. Bureau of the Census, *SAUS: 1980,* p. 454, Table 752.

66. The literature supporting such views is summarized in Anderson, *Welfare,* pp. 133–151. A guaranteed-income program would likely reach a greater percentage of Americans in poverty than the current programs and would also reduce the bureaucratic tangles that recipients of aid now sometimes face. However, under the guaranteed-income approach, if each individual family of four was guaranteed an income of $4,000 and the family's subsidy was reduced by 25 cents for every additional dollar it earned beyond $4,000 (an effective tax rate of 25 percent added on top of that of other income taxes and social security), the family would continue to receive public money until its income reached $16,000. That is, under such a plan, each such American family with an income below $16,000 would receive public money. The example suggests that an effective guaranteed-income plan would cost in excess of the programs currently in effect, possibly considerably in excess.

67. See Robert G. Spiegelman and K. E. Yaeger, "Overview" (The Seattle and Denver Income Maintenance Experiments), *Journal of Human Resources* 15, no. 4 (Fall 1980), pp. 463–79; Henry Aaron and John Todd, "The Use of Income Maintenance Experiment Findings in Public Policy, 1977–78," *Proceedings of the Thirty-First Annual Meeting,* Industrial Relations Research Association, 1979, pp. 46–56; Robinson G. Hollister, "Welfare Reform and Labor Markets: What Have We Learned from the Experiments?" *Proceedings of the Thirty-First Annual Meeting,* Industrial Relations Research

Association, 1979, pp. 57–70; Joseph A. Pechman and Michael P. Timpane, eds., *Work Incentives and Income Guarantees: The New Jersey Negative Income Tax Experiment* (Washington, D.C.: Brookings, 1975).

68. Nor should we ignore that the alternatives may well have unintended negative consequences as serious as those of the current policies. As an example, see note 28, above.

69. Council on Environmental Quality, *Environmental Quality, 1973* (Washington, D.C.: U.S. Government Printing Office, 1973), p. 78, Table 1.

70. Based on figures reported in U.S. Senate, Committee on Public Works, Subcommittee on Air and Water Pollution, "Air Pollution—1966," 89th Cong. (1966), pp. 270–71.

71. Allen V. Kneese and Charles L. Schultz, *Pollution, Prices, and Public Policy* (Washington, D.C.: Brookings, 1975), p. 50.

72. James E. Anderson et al., *Public Policy and Politics In America* (North Scituate, Mass.: Duxbury Press, 1978), p. 76.

73. U.S. Environmental Protection Agency, *Trends in the Quality of the Nation's Air* (Washington, D.C.: U.S. Government Printing Office, 1980), p. 5, Graph A.

74. Ibid., p. 7, Graph A.

75. Figures for the 1970s are found in ibid., p. 5, Graph A; p. 7, Graph A; p. 9, Graph B; p. 11, Graph A; and p. 12, Graph A.

76. Lester B. Lave and Gilbert S. Omenn, *Cleaning the Air: Reforming the Clean Air Act* (Washington, D.C.: Brookings, 1981), p. 21, note 44.

77. The 1973–74 and 1979–80 figures for days of hazardous and unhealthful pollution in urban areas are found in Council on Environmental Quality, *Environmental Quality, 1981* (Washington, D.C.: U.S. Government Printing Office, 1982), pp. 244–45.

78. Ibid.

79. Ibid., p. 33, Figure 2-3.

80. U.S. Department of Commerce, *Environmental Statistics, 1978,* p. 102.

81. Council on Environmental Quality, *Environmental Quality, 1980* (Washington, D.C.: U.S. Government Printing Office, 1981), p. 100.

82. Based on figures reported in Council on Environmental Quality, *Environmental Quality, 1979* (Washington, D.C.: U.S Government Printing Office, 1980), pp. 90–91. A rise or fall in the violation rate by 10 percent or greater was considered a noticeable change.

83. *Christian Science Monitor,* May 5, 1981.

84. *Christian Science Monitor,* April 2, 1980.

85. Council on Environmental Quality, *Environmental Quality, 1979,* pp. 654–55, and p. 666, Table 12-4. Regulation may also have indirect costs, such as its possible impact on prices (inflation) and on worker productivity, which are discussed in Chapter 3.

86. Ibid, p. 655.

87. On this point, see Appendix.

88. For an elaboration of this general conclusion, see David Harrison, Jr., and Paul R. Portney, "Making Ready for the Clean Air Act," *AEI Journal on Government and Society* (April 1981), pp. 24–31.

89. *Time Magazine,* September 29, 1980, p. 57.

90. All figures on waste in this and the following paragraph are taken or calculated from Republican Study Committee, House of Representatives, *Special Report: Waste, Fraud, Abuse and Mismanagement In the Federal Government* (Rosslyn, Va.: The Fund for a Conservative Majority, 1980).

91. Republican Study Committee, *Special Report,* p. 27 (items 25, 26, 27, 28, 29, 31, 32); p. 28 (items 46, 47, 48); p. 29 (items 51, 53, 56, 58, 59); p. 30 (items 60, 62, 64, 67, 68, 69, 70); p. 31 (items 72, 74, 75, 78, 79, 80, 81); p. 32 (items 83, 86, 89, 90, 93); p. 33 (items 97, 98, 103, 104, 105, 106, 107).

92. The findings of the report and future projections are reported in *Christian Science Monitor,* August 3, 1981.

93. *Christian Science Monitor,* April 10, 1981.

94. An average day amounts to somewhat more than ten hours, not including work on weekends. See Charles O. Jones, *The United States Congress: People, Place and Policy* (Homewood, Ill.: Dorsey Press, 1982), pp. 18–43; Ross Webber, "U.S. Senators: See How They Run," *Wharton Magazine* (Winter 1980–81), p. 37; John S. Saloma III, *Congress and the New Politics* (Boston: Little, Brown, 1969), pp. 184–85.

95. U.S. Chamber of Commerce, *Handbook on White Collar Crime: Everyone's Problem, Everyone's Loss* (Washington, D.C.: U.S. Chamber of Commerce, 1974), p. 6.

96. Inventory shortages resulting from employee theft in department stores and specialty chains alone amount to almost $5 billion annually, according to "But That Would Be Wrong," *Psychology Today* (November 1981), p. 50. "Employee theft is *twice* as important a source of loss as is shoplifting," p. 50 (emphasis added).

97. United States productivity figures are found in U.S. Department of Labor, *Handbook of Labor Statistics* (Washington, D.C.: U.S. Government Printing Office, 1980), p. 206, Table 104 (for nonfarm business employees) and p. 230, Table 106 (for employees of government programs).

### 3 The Political Legacy of the 1960s and 1970s

1. This was a view of not only conservatives but also an array of former leading liberal spokesmen. On this point, see Peter Steinfels, *The Neoconservatives: The Men Who Are Changing America's Politics* (New York: Simon & Schuster, 1979), pp. 58–63.

2. William Simon, *A Time for Truth* (New York: McGraw-Hill, 1978); George Gilder, *Wealth and Poverty* (New York: Basic Books, 1981); Milton Friedman and Rose Friedman, *Free to Choose* (New York: Avon, 1979); E. S. Savas, *Privatis-*

*ing the Public Sector* (Chatham, N.J.: Chatham House, 1982); Herbert Stein, "Balancing the Budget," in William Fellner, ed., *Contemporary Economic Problems, 1979* (Washington, D.C.: American Enterprise Institute, 1979), pp. 191–231; Gottfried Haberler, "The Present Economic Malaise," in Fellner, ed., *Contemporary Economic Problems, 1979*, pp. 261–90; Jude Wanniski, *The Way the World Works: How Economies Fail—and Succeed* (New York: Basic Books, 1978); William Bowen, "Ailing Productivity," *Fortune,* December 3, 1979, pp. 68–80; Murray L. Weidenbaum, *The Future of Government Regulation* (New York: Amacom, 1979); as well as Ronald Reagan, "Inaugural Address," in Ellis Sandoz and Cecil V. Crabb, Jr., eds., *A Tide of Discontent* (Washington, D.C.: Congressional Quarterly Press, 1981), pp. 211–16.

3. *Time Magazine,* September 14, 1981, p. 15.

4. Representative examples are the references in note 2.

5. In 1960, for example, individual income, corporate profit, and property taxes at all levels of government totaled 73 percent of all government general revenue taxation; in 1979, they totaled 76 percent. U.S. Bureau of the Census, *Statistical Abstract of the United States, 1981* (Washington, D.C.: U.S. Government Printing Office, 1981), p. 280, Table 473; hereafter cited as Bureau of the Census, *SAUS.*

6. Corporate profits taxes 1950–80 for federal and state governments are in Bureau of the Census, *SAUS: 1972,* p. 482, Table 773 (for 1950 and 1955); *SAUS: 1980,* p. 573, Table 963 (for 1960–79). The figures are reported without inventory valuation adjustments and capital depreciation allowances. When these are added, corporate taxes as a percentage of profits declined by about 3 percent between 1960 and 1979.

An unresolved controversy exists over how much the reported incomes of corporations are artificially overstated and thus overtaxed because of inflation. During inflationary periods, for example, the real cost of replacing such capital items as structures and machinery becomes substantially greater than the price at which the items were originally purchased.

222

However, the companies are allowed to base their reported depreciation costs only on the price originally paid rather than on the current, actual price of replacement. With depreciation costs stated at an artificially lower level than the real replacement price, the overall income corporations report becomes that much higher. In this manner a period of inflation can artificially increase the reported income of corporations and, by the same token, the taxes they pay.

A number of economists have found that the effects of inflation work both ways and almost exactly cancel out each other with respect to corporate taxes. The work of these economists indicates that inflation has not artificially increased the taxes corporations pay. Some other economists have found differently. But a leading proponent of this latter view, Martin Feldstein, reaches his conclusion at least in part because he excludes the effects of the various corporate tax changes that have taken place over the years. He does so on the premise that the tax changes had the purpose of spurring investment rather than adjusting for inflation. For the different viewpoints on this issue, see Nicholas J. Gonedes, "Evidence on the 'Tax Effects' of Inflation Under Historical Cost Accounting Methods," *Journal of Business* 54, no. 2 (April 1981), pp. 227–71; Phillip Cagan and Robert Lipsey, *The Financial Effects of Inflation* (New York: Ballinger, 1978); John Shoven and Jeremy Bulow, "Inflation Accounting and Nonfinancial Corporate Profits: Financial Assets and Liabilities," *Brookings Papers on Economic Activity*, no. 1 (Washington, D.C.: Brookings, 1978); and Martin Feldstein and Lawrence Summers, "Inflation and the Taxation of Capital Income in the Corporate Sector," *National Tax Journal* (December 1979), pp. 445–71.

7. *Christian Science Monitor*, August 26, 1980, p. 14.

8. Findings for 1960–75 suggest that the marginal tax rate on corporate income from capital, depending upon how measured, either remained steady or declined by as much as 5 percent over the period. See Douglas H. Joines, "Estimates of

Effective Marginal Tax Rates on Factor Incomes," *Journal of Business* 54, no. 2 (April 1981), p. 204, Table 3.

9. Bureau of the Census, *SAUS: 1981,* p. 280, Table 473 (federal and state, 1960–80); *SAUS: 1965,* p. 420, Table 566 (federal and state, 1950 and 1955). Since the figures include corporate taxes, local income taxes are excluded. Figures for personal income in the nation, upon which to determine income taxation as a percentage of personal income, are in Bureau of the Census, *SAUS: 1981,* p. 427, Table 713 (for 1960–80); *SAUS: 1965,* p. 331, Table 455 (for 1950 and 1955).

10. Figures in the following three paragraphs are from Bureau of the Census, *SAUS: 1980,* p. 272, Table 455; *SAUS: 1965,* p. 400, Table 538.

11. Examining total income tax payments relative to income allows a measure of the changes in the overall burden the government places on the public. While concern about the government's overall size lies at the core of our inquiry, another matter, standing somewhat apart from the question of overall size, involves the level at which the government taxes our last dollar of income, or the marginal tax rate. For example, the government could decide to tax our last dollar of earnings more and our first dollar less, which would, in effect, increase the marginal tax rate but not change the overall tax as a percentage of overall income. The question here focuses especially on the individual taxpayer's incentive to earn more income as he or she faces a higher marginal tax on the next dollar earned. It is thought that raising the marginal rate of tax on the last dollar earned would reduce the incentive of people to work harder and earn more. However, it is far from proven that a higher marginal tax rate on the last dollar of income earned or received does affect economic behavior negatively. Presumably, the theory is valid in some cases. But some individuals facing higher marginal tax rates might equally decide to work harder and earn *more* than they would have otherwise in order to be able to keep the after-tax style of living to which they have grown accustomed or to

gain the higher living standard to which they aspire. In these cases, raising the marginal tax rate would stimulate more rather than less work.

As for evidence about changes in federal marginal income-tax rates, examination of tax information suggests that marginal rates did not alter dramatically from 1960 through 1979 for the large majority of taxpayers. Relatively few married taxpayers and hardly any single taxpayers consistently had to pay a markedly larger marginal rate of tax from 1975–1980 than would have been paid in 1960 on the same real income. However, some notable exceptions do exist. These exceptions are people at income levels for which the marginal rate of tax throughout the 1975–80 period was 5 percent or more above the marginal tax that would have been paid at the beginning of the 1960s on the same real income. The exceptions include married couples with children who earned about $30,000 or more in 1979 and married couples with no children who earned above $25,000 in 1979, both groups together comprising about 13 percent of the American taxpayers. Generally, for single individuals, the marginal tax rate at these income levels did not change appreciably from 1960–80. A narrowing in this discrepancy between the taxes paid by married and unmarried taxpayers earning above $25,000 a year is now in process. For the tax figures, see U.S. Bureau of the Census, *SAUS: 1981,* p. 260, Table 443.

12. Property tax figures for California and the United States in 1977 are from Bureau of the Census, *SAUS: 1979,* p. 306, Table 502; *SAUS: 1972,* p. 409, Table 649 (for the United States, 1950–70), and p. 418, Table 661 (for California in 1970, calculated from per capita figures). Figures for personal income in the nation and California, upon which to determine property tax as a percentage of personal income, are in the Bureau of the Census, *SAUS: 1978,* p. 448, Table 724 (for California and the United States for 1977); *SAUS: 1972,* p. 319, Table 519 (for California in 1970 and the United States 1950–70).

13. The OECD figures in the following paragraph are reported in Bureau of the Census, *SAUS: 1981*, p. 880, Table 1556.

14. Figures on total governmental revenues and on GNP, from which to determine total revenues as a percentage of GNP, are from President of the United States, *Economic Report of the President* (Washington, D.C.: U.S. Government Printing Office, 1981), p. 233, Table B-1 (column 1), and p. 318, Table B-73 (column 1).

15. Figures for social insurance taxes and contributions are in Bureau of the Census, *SAUS: 1980*, p. 260, Table 434 (for 1960 through 1979). Figures for GNP, upon which to determine social insurance taxes as a percentage of GNP, are in Bureau of the Census, *SAUS: 1980*, p. 439, Table 725 (for 1960–80).

16. Figures on the federal deficit cited in the following paragraph are from Bureau of the Census, *SAUS: 1980*, p. 258, Table 430 (for 1970 through 1979); figures on gross national product, upon which to determine the deficit as a percentage of GNP, are in Bureau of the Census, *SAUS: 1980* p. 437, Table 724.

17. Figures on outstanding private mortgage and consumer debt cited in the following paragraph are from Bureau of the Census, *SAUS: 1980*, p. 540, Tables 893 and 894, and *SAUS: 1979*, p. 537, Tables 876 and 877. Figures on outstanding federal debt are from Bureau of the Census, *SAUS: 1980*, p. 258, Table 430.

18. Figures for budget deficits cited in the following paragraph are found in United Nations, Department of Economic and Social Affairs, *Statistical Yearbook: 1978* (New York: United Nations, 1979), p. 818, Table 201, for the United States; p. 836, Table 201, for Japan; p. 860, Table 201, for West Germany (the 1978 West German deficit is in Statistisches Bundesamt, *Statistisches Jahrbuch, 1980 für die Bundesrepublik Deutschland* [Wiesbaden, 1980], p. 400, Table 19.4). Figures for gross domestic product, upon which to determine deficits

as a percentage of GNP, are from United Nations, *Statistical Yearbook, 1978*, p. 707, Table 185, for the United States; p. 704, Table 185, for West Germany; p. 705, Table 185, for Japan.

19. George L. Perry, "Slowing the Wage-Price Spiral: The Macroeconomic View," in Arthur M. Okun and George L. Perry, eds., *Curing Chronic Inflation* (Washington, D.C.: Brookings, 1978), pp. 43–45.

20. U.S. Cong., Congressional Budget Office, *The Fiscal Policy Response to Inflation*, Report to the Senate and House Committees on the Budget (January 1979), pt. 1, pp. 42–44; Congressional Budget Office, *Entering the 1980s: Fiscal Policy Choices*, Report to the Senate and House Committees on the Budget (January 1980), p. 90.

21. The figures in the following paragraph on government employees and total nonagricultural employment in the nation are based on Bureau of the Census, *SAUS: 1980*, pp. 413–15, Table 692, for 1979; *SAUS: 1972*, pp. 227–29, Table 364, for 1960.

22. Weidenbaum, *The Future of Government Regulation*, p. 23.

23. Weidenbaum calculated the 1976 regulatory costs at $65.5 billion in "The Costs of Government Regulation of Business," Joint Economic Committee, U.S. Cong., April 10, 1978, p. 16.

24. Ronald Reagan, "Report to the Nation on the Economy," broadcast, February 5, 1981, in Sandoz and Crabb, Jr., eds., *A Tide of Discontent*, p. 217.

25. Haberler, "The Present Economic Malaise," pp. 278–79.

26. *Christian Science Monitor*, June 9, 1981, p. 22.

27. The results of the poll are found in U.S. Cong., Joint Economic Committee, Subcommittee on Economic Growth and Stabilization, "The Cost of Government Regulation," April 11–13, 1978, p. 82.

28. The following seven paragraphs are based on the

sources cited in notes 22 and 23 and on Tables 1 and 2 of this chapter.

29. Dr. Weidenbaum's widely publicized result of $65.5 billion in regulatory costs for 1976 (Table 1) amounts to 3.8 percent of the 1976 GNP. The total for 1976 (Table 2), $54.6 billion, or 3.2 percent of the 1976 GNP, differs from the aforementioned $65.5 billion solely as an artifact of the different base (administrative cost) figures to be found in different places in Dr. Weidenbaum's own work. All of the base figures in Table 2 are those of Dr. Weidenbaum.

30. John W. Kendrick, "International Comparisons of Recent Productivity Trends," in William Fellner, ed., *Essays in Contemporary Economic Problems* (Washington, D.C.: American Enterprise Institute, 1981), pp. 154–56.

31. Ibid., pp. 140–41, Table 7.

32. The Data Resources and Chase Econometrics conclusions are reported in "Fighting Regulation with Cost and Benefit Analyses," *Congressional Quarterly Weekly,* February 17, 1979, pp. 285–86.

33. Figures on investment for the period from 1950 through 1979 are in Bureau of the Census, *SAUS: 1980,* p. 439, Table 725, and *1967,* p. 321, Table 455, for nonresidential investment; Bureau of the Census, *SAUS: 1980,* p. 562, Table 940, and *1965,* p. 501, Table 690, for new plant and equipment; Bureau of the Census, *SAUS: 1980,* p. 809, Table 1444, and *1967,* p. 755, Table 1126, for manufacturers' capital purchases. Figures for GNP in the nation, from which forms of investment as a percentage of GNP are calculated, are found in Bureau of the Census, *SAUS: 1980,* p. 437, Table 724. For yearly investment as a percentage of GNP from 1950 to 1980, see "Public Policy and Capital Formation," *Federal Reserve Bulletin* 67, no. 10 (October 1981), p. 749, Graph 1.

34. The net stock of capital, or net investment, is the difference between the formation of new capital and the depreciation of old capital. From 1950 through 1959, net nonresidential

investment (net stock of fixed nonresidential private capital) in constant dollars increased by just over 40 percent; from 1970 through 1979, the increase in net nonresidential investment was about 37 percent in constant dollars. See U.S. Department of Commerce, *Survey of Current Business,* February 1981, p. 60, Table 4.

35. Figures on manufacturing productivity in the following paragraph are based on Bureau of the Census, *SAUS: 1980,* p. 416, Table 693, for 1960 through 1979, and *1970,* p. 229, Table 338, for 1950–60.

36. Indeed, in the ten years of the 1970s American productivity rose by 40 percent or more in such varied industries as air transport and aerospace, aluminum rolling, major household appliances, paints and allied products, synthetic fibers, and telecommunications. See Bureau of the Census, *SAUS: 1981,* p. 399, Table 670.

37. The nation's balance of trade in manufactured goods with foreign nations did not change dramatically from 1970 to 1980, or fall deeply into the negative, as is often presumed. To the contrary, our trade balance in manufactured goods with foreign countries stayed the same from 1970 through 1979, remaining positive by about $4 billion at both the beginning and the end of the period. It rose to a positive $18 billion in 1980. Also contrary to common impression, the exchange rate of the dollar did not fall steeply relative to the combined currencies of our trading partners. Depending on the measure chosen, the value of the dollar remained generally steady according to the bilateral trade-weighted average of our trading partners' currencies and slipped by approximately 10 percent according to the multilateral trade-weighted average. See, President of the United States, *Economic Report of the President,* 1981, p. 343, Table B-98 (for the exchange rates) and p. 348, Table B-102 (for the trade balances in manufactured goods).

38. The following figures on civilian employment are based on Bureau of the Census, *SAUS: 1980,* p. 396, Table 655, for

1960 to 1980, and *1967,* p. 221, Table 314, for 1950–60.

39. The number of Americans employed in full-time jobs the whole year long rose by 50 percent more in the 1970s compared with the 1950s. Nor were the jobs created during the 1970s disproportionately in fast-food chains, the clerical field, or other like endeavors, as some might imagine. During the 1970s, managerial and administrative jobs climbed by almost 3 million, or by 36 percent. Professional and technical jobs (accountants, doctors, engineers, lawyers, nurses, scientists, social workers, and teachers) rose by 4 million, again a 36 percent increase. On its part, work in the food service industry grew by about 1 million jobs, also a 36 percent increase. Jobs in clerical work climbed by 4 million over the period, a rise of 27 percent. See Bureau of the Census, *SAUS: 1981,* p. 402, Table 675.

40. Figures on growth of real GNP from 1950 through 1959 and from 1970 through 1979 are calculated from President of the United States, *Economic Report of the President, 1981,* p. 234, Table B-2. Recall that yearly averages are expressed in simple, not compound, terms.

41. Comparative figures on the rate of growth in industrial production for 1970 through 1979 are in President of the United States, *Economic Report of the President, 1981,* p. 354, Table B-108.

42. The following figures on real personal disposable income are based on Bureau of the Census, *SAUS: 1980,* p. 440, Table 729, and *SAUS: 1976,* p. 396, Table 634.

43. Bureau of the Census, *SAUS: 1980,* p. 796, Table 1415, and p. 651, Table 1119. From one-half to three-quarters of the advances in the ownership of various products occurred after 1970.

44. Bureau of the Census, *SAUS: 1981,* p. 763, Table 1377.

45. Robert B. Reich, "The Next American Frontier," *The Atlantic,* March, 1983, p. 44.

46. Recall, too, that the nation's manufacturing sector, taken as a whole, generally retained its competitiveness in

the international marketplace throughout these years. For documentation, see this chapter's note 37.

## 4 How False Images Became Accepted Doctrine

1. A dramatic change in popular opinion about government took place over the 1960–80 period, occurring mainly in the Vietnam and Watergate years of 1965–74. Of note, however, is that popular confidence in government never rose above its Vietnam and Watergate nadir throughout the rest of the decade. Not even the slightest improvement occurred, according to both the Survey Research Center and the Harris polls. In fact, by numerous measures, confidence dropped even lower from 1974 to 1980. For example, popular trust in Congress declined precipitously, indeed plummeting more rapidly after 1973 than it had before; also, the public's confidence in the government to do what is right and the public's feeling that governmental officials knew what they were doing both declined following 1974. Finally, the feeling that the government doesn't care what happens to individual Americans and that the government wastes a lot of taxpayers' money continued to increase in the second half of the 1970s.

The opinion results for 1980 are obtainable from Warren E. Miller and the National Election Studies Center for Political Studies, *The American National Election Study, 1980* (Ann Arbor, Mich.: 1982), vol. 1, pp. 220–21. Figures for earlier years are in Warren E. Miller et al., *American National Election Studies Data Sourcebook, 1952–1978* (Cambridge, Mass.: Harvard University Press, 1980), p. 257; the figures on the public's confidence in Congress are from David B. Hill and Norman R. Luttbeg, *Trends in American Electoral Behavior* (Itasca, Ill.: Peacock, 1980), p. 122.

2. Edward R. Tufte, *Political Control of the Economy* (Princeton, N.J.: Princeton University Press, 1978); Gerald H. Kramer, "Short-term Fluctuations in U.S. Voting Behavior, 1896–1964," *American Political Science Review* 65 (1971), pp.

131–43; Morris P. Fiorina, *Retrospective Voting in American National Elections* (New Haven, Conn.: Yale University Press, 1981).

3. For a representative sample of spokesmen holding this general view and a selection of their writings, see Chapter 3, note 2.

4. The evidence for each of the statements found in the following three paragraphs has been presented in the text and notes of Chapter 3.

5. Explorations of the pressures on American life resulting from the baby boom in the United States are contained, for example, in Richard A. Easterlin, *Birth and Fortune: The Impact of Numbers on Personal Welfare* (New York: Basic Books, 1980), and idem, *Population, Labor Force, and Long Swings in Economic Growth* (New York: Columbia University Press, 1968); Landon Y. Jones, *Great Expectations: America and the Baby Boom Generation* (New York: Coward, McCann, and Geoghegan, 1980). But even these authors do not focus on the conjunction of the baby boom with the change in attitude among women toward entering the work force and the increasing rate of marital separations and divorce, all of which combine to form what I call the crowded generation.

6. Figures on birth rates and on total births presented in the following paragraph are from United Nations, *Demographic Yearbook* (New York: United Nations, annual); for birth rates 1930–65, see *1965,* Table 12; for live births 1946–65, see *1965,* Table 11; for live births covering the 1930s through 1945, see *1948,* Table 13, and to correct for underregistration of births, see U.S. Bureau of the Census, *Statistical Abstract of the United States, 1953* (Washington, D.C.: U.S. Government Printing Office, 1953), p. 63, Table 56, hereafter cited as Bureau of the Census, *SAUS.*

7. Figures on marital status and divorce rates 1940–80 are found in Bureau of the Census, *SAUS: 1980* p. 61, Table 85.

8. The following labor force figures for 1950–80 are from

President of the United States, *Economic Report of the President, 1981* (Washington, D.C.: U.S. Government Printing Office, 1981), pp. 264–65, Table B-27.

9. Birth rates of below 20 per 1,000 adults were typical in West Germany from immediately after World War II, in France after 1950, and in Japan after 1954; in contrast, the birth rate in the United States remained at more than 20 per 1,000 adults until 1965 with no respite at all. Our birth rate exceeded that of West Germany on average by about 30 percent and that of France by about 20 percent from 1946 to 1965 and that of Japan on average by about 25 percent from 1951 to 1965. While Japan's birth rate from 1946 to 1951 was higher than ours, even then (unlike ours) it did not reflect a change in birth rate from the prewar decade. For birth rates over the 1930–65 period, see United Nations, *Demographic Yearbook, 1965* (New York: United Nations, 1966), Table 12.

10. Comparative figures on the size of labor forces are in Bureau of the Census, *SAUS: 1981,* p. 882, Table 1560.

11. Kay Lehman Schlozman and Sidney Verba, *Injury to Insult* (Cambridge, Mass.: Harvard University Press, 1979), p. 40, Table 2-5.

12. Ibid.

13. The number of employed Americans rose by 21 percent between 1950 and 1965, or from 58.9 million to 71.1 million. Had the nation maintained the same rate of increase in employment (21 percent) from 1965 to 1980, by 1980 there would have been 86 million Americans employed. The total civilian labor force in the middle of 1980 was 104.5 million Americans, or 18.5 million more than 86 million.

14. In the five years between 1965 and 1970, net borrowing climbed by 15 percent relative to the nation's GNP, compared with a growth rate of 12.4 percent between 1960 and 1965. Four-fifths of the increase in outstanding debt after 1965 was due to increased private borrowing; one-fifth was the responsibility of increased public borrowing. Figures on private debt, public debt, and the GNP upon which to calculate

changes in debt as a percentage are from Bureau of the Census, *SAUS: 1975,* p. 381, Table 616 (GNP), and p. 473, Table 764 (public and private outstanding debt).

15. The following is calculated from figures for productivity per hour (nonfarm business, all persons) and real hourly compensation per person in nonfarm business, in U.S. Department of Labor, *Handbook of Labor Statistics* (Washington, D.C.: U.S. Government Printing Office, 1980), p. 206, Table 104.

16. This and the following inflation figures are from President of the United States, *Economic Report of the President,* p. 293, Table B-53.

17. Oil prices increased sharply during the final quarter of 1973 and rose beyond 10 percent also in 1974, 1975, 1979, and 1980.

18. Services and related occupations rose from about 40 million to 64 million employees from 1965 to 1980; manufacturing and related occupations rose from 22 million to 26 million employees during the same period. See Bureau of the Census, *SAUS: 1980,* p. 411, Table 689, section on goods-related and services-related employment.

19. William Bowen, "Better Prospects for Our Ailing Productivity," *Fortune,* December 3, 1979, pp. 68–83, esp. p. 74.

20. The age composition of the employed labor force changed markedly. In 1960, 18.3 percent of employed Americans were age 55 or over and 14.3 percent were under the age of 25; by 1979, 14.8 percent were age 55 and over and 22.5 percent were under the age of 25. The percentage of employed Americans under the age of 25 increased by half from 1960 to 1980.

21. Mark Perlman, "Some Economic Consequences of the New Patterns of Population Growth," in William Fellner, ed., *Contemporary Economic Problems* (Washington, D.C.: American Enterprise Institute, 1981), p. 263. For the change in age structure of supervisorial personnel, see Mark Perlman, "One Man's Baedeker to Productivity Growth Discussions," in William Fellner, ed., *Contemporary Economic Problems,*

*1979* (Washington, D.C.: American Enterprise Institute, 1979), pp. 108–111.

22. John W. Kendrick, "Productivity Trends and the Recent Slowdown," in Fellner, ed., *Contemporary Economic Problems, 1979,* p. 33, Table 4; Bowen, "Better Prospects for Our Ailing Productivity," p. 74.

23. Bowen, "Better Prospects for Our Ailing Productivity,' pp. 69–70.

24. Figures on numbers of families and unrelated individuals for 1952–80 are in President of the United States, *Economic Report of the President,* p. 262, Table B-25. Figures for 1950 are in Bureau of the Census, *SAUS: 1951,* p. 25, Table 32.

25. Although tempting now to view inflation as out of control during the post-Eisenhower period, recall that only once did the rate of inflation move beyond even 7 percent during the period except for the years of stiff oil price increases.

## 5 Public Opinion and the Public Programs of Government

1. *Gallup Political Index,* April 1966, Report 11, p. 7. Persons holding no opinion were excluded.

2. Ibid.

3. The following poll results are from George H. Gallup, *The Gallup Poll: Public Opinion, 1935–1971* (New York: Random House, 1972), vol. 3: on priorities, pp. 1700–01; on job programs for unemployed youths, pp. 1732, 1762, 1838, 1897; on medical programs for the elderly, pp. 1721, 1915; and on the priority given to such programs, pp. 1700–01.

4. Louis Harris and Associates, *The Harris Survey Yearbook of Public Opinion, 1970* (New York: Louis Harris and Associates, 1971), p. 48.

5. Louis Harris and Associates, *The Harris Survey Yearbook of Public Opinion, 1972* (New York: Louis Harris and Associates, 1976), p. 141.

6. The Gallup results are reported in Table 4.

7. Harris, *The Harris Survey, 1972,* p. 141.

8. Gallup, *The Gallup Poll*, vol. 3, p. 2177 (question 10b).

9. The following results are reported in Gallup, *The Gallup Poll*, p. 2193 (on food stamps); *Gallup Political Index*, November 1970, p. 26; and William Watts and Lloyd A. Free, *State of the Nation* (New York: Universe Books, 1973), pp. 295–96.

10. Richard M. Scammon and Ben J. Wattenberg, *The Real Majority* (New York: Coward-McCann, 1970), p. 76.

11. Martin Anderson, *Welfare* (Stanford, Calif.: Stanford University Press, 1978), p. 63. Three polls were taken by Gallup on the matter from 1965 through 1970, the year in which Congress defeated the administration's guaranteed-income proposal. According to each of these polls, between 58 percent and 67 percent of the public opposed the guaranteed-income concept; not once did as much as 40 percent of the public support it. See Gallup, *The Gallup Poll*, vol. 3, pp. 1965, 2133–34, and 2177.

12. William Watts and Lloyd A. Free, *State of the Nation, III* (Lexington, Mass.: Lexington Books, 1978), pp. 215–16, items 14 g and j; 15 d, e, and f.

13. Anderson, *Welfare*, pp. 59–66.

14. U.S. Bureau of the Census, *Statistical Abstract of the United States: 1980* (Washington, D.C.: U.S. Government Printing Office, 1980), p. 329, Table 530.

15. Ibid.

16. See Chapter 3, Table 2.

17. Timothy Clark, "New Approaches to Regulatory Reform," *National Journal*, August 11, 1979, p. 1317.

18. The polls cited in this paragraph are found in Harris, *The Harris Survey, 1970*, pp. 48–49.

19. Harris, *The Harris Survey, 1972*, p. 137.

20. The results of numerous polling organizations demonstrate the continued presence of popular favor for environmental controls throughout the decade of the 1970s. A compilation of polling results from many sources, including the Roper polls, is found in Council on Environmental Quality,

*Environmental Quality, 1980* (Washington, D.C.: U.S. Government Printing Office, 1980), p. 405, Figure 1, and pp. 406–7. A poll not cited there, the "State of the Nation" poll by Potomac Associates and Gallup in 1976, concluded similarly. It found "unmistakable public support for *increased* spending to reduce water and air pollution" (emphasis in original) and that air and water pollution control constituted one of the top priorities among Americans. Watts and Free, *State of the Nation, III*, p. 93.

21. The results of Harris, Roper, and the National Opinion Research Corporation polls on this topic are found in Council on Environmental Quality, *Environmental Quality, 1980*, p. 406.

## 6 The Present and the Past

1. See Chapter 1 above, and note 6.

2. Ronnie Dugger, *On Reagan: The Man and His Presidency* (New York: McGraw-Hill, 1983), p. 109.

3. Ibid., p. 292.

4. Based on Gregory B. Mills, "The Budget: A Failure of Discipline," in John L. Palmer and Isabel V. Sawhill, eds., *The Reagan Record: An Assessment of America's Changing Domestic Priorities* (Cambridge, Mass.: Ballinger, 1984), pp. 110 and 112–13. The increase in defense spending during the Reagan era is above and beyond the increase already projected in 1980.

5. For the changes in marginal tax rates from 1981 to 1985 in constant dollars, see Bureau of the Census, *SAUS: 1986*, p. 319, Table 517. Marginal taxes fell by one-tenth, from 28 to 25 percent, for Americans with average family incomes, from 44 to 38 percent for families with incomes of $50,000, and from 54 to 42 percent for families with incomes above $75,000. The figures used refer to married couples with children.

6. Perry D. Quick, "Businesses: Reagan's Industrial Policy," in Palmer and Sawhill, *The Reagan Record,* pp. 300 and 302.

7. For 1977, Sheldon H. Danziger and Daniel H. Weinberg, *Fighting Poverty: What Works and What Doesn't* (Cambridge, Mass.: Harvard University Press, 1986), p. 229; for 1980 and 1985, James Gwartney, "New Directions in Antipoverty Policy: Lessons from the Past and Guidance for the Future," in U.S. Congress, Joint Economic Committee, *A Symposium on the 40th Anniversary of the Joint Economic Committee*, 99th Cong., 2nd sess., January 16–17, 1986, p. 607.

8. Gwartney, "New Directions in Antipoverty Policy," p. 607. From 1980 to 1984 the total amount spent on all means-tested programs fell by $1 billion, to $80.3 billion.

9. Danziger and Weinberg, *Fighting Poverty*, p. 35, Figure 2.3.

10. Quick, "Businesses," p. 309, projections for a five-year period, based on the "Report of the President's Task Force on Regulatory Relief," August 1983.

11. Lou Cannon, *Reagan* (New York: Putnam, 1982), p. 321.

12. President Reagan himself agrees that his presidency secured the enactment and implementation of a new direction of policy. Speaking in mid-1984 of his first term in office, Reagan observed: "America began a fundamental change in policy direction in 1981; a change from a policy of government promises, a change from taxing you more no matter how hard you tried, to rewarding you for working harder and producing more. Personal incentives are changing America, restoring our spirit, strengthening our economy." Ronald Reagan, "Radio Address to the Nation," June 23, 1984, in General Services Administration, *Weekly Compilation of Presidential Documents*, Administration of Ronald Reagan, July 2, 1984, p. 931.

13. Calculated through 1983 from Sheldon H. Danziger et al., "Antipoverty Policy: Effects on the Poor and the Nonpoor," in Danziger and Weinberg, *Fighting Poverty*, p. 54, column on pretransfer poverty.

14. Refer to Graph 1 for sources.

15. U.S. Department of Commerce, Bureau of the Census,

*Money, Income, and Poverty Status of Families and Persons of the United States, 1984,* August 27, 1985; and Robert Greenstein, "Hard Choices: Federal Budget Priorities in the Gramm-Rudman-Hollings Era," Center on Budget and Policy Priorities, June 1986, p. 13.

16. David Kahan and Keith McKeown, "New Census Data Show Widening Income Gap Between Wealthiest and Other Americans," Center on Budget and Policy Priorities, August 6, 1986, Table 1, based on U.S. Department of Commerce, Bureau of the Census, *After-Tax Money Income Estimates of Households for 1984* (1986). Had public assistance not been enlarged from 1960 to 1980, a marked widening of the income gap between the rich and the poor would also have occurred in those years. See Joseph A. Pechman, *The Rich, the Poor, and the Taxes They Pay* (Brighton, Eng.: Wheatsheaf Books, 1986), pp. 22–23, 25–26, 29.

17. Marilyn Moon and Isabel V. Sawhill, "Family Incomes: Gainers and Losers," in Palmer and Sawhill, *The Reagan Record,* pp. 321–22.

18. A survey by the Conference of Mayors of cities and towns found that even in the second year of the recovery (1984), the need for emergency food assistance had risen over 1983 in nearly 75 percent of the municipalities, leading to a rise by 50 percent in the one year alone in the total number of meals provided. See J. Larry Brown, "Hunger in the U.S.," *Scientific American* 256, no. 2 (February 1987), p. 37.

19. Infant mortality among blacks, which had been declining annually at a rate of 1.1 per 1,000 births from 1965 to 1980 —including a decline of 1.0 per 1,000 births from 1975 to 1980 and from 1980 to 1982—dropped to a decline of only 0.6 per 1,000 births after 1982. This slower rate of decline after 1982 parallels the slower rate of decline that existed prior to 1965. Infant mortality rates through 1982 are found in Bureau of the Census, *SAUS: 1986,* p. 72, Table 112. For the period through 1984, see U.S. Department of Health and Human Services, Public Health Service, Center for Disease Control, "Morbid-

ity and Mortality Weekly Report," January 16, 1987, p. 1.

20. Thomas J. Main, "The Homeless Families of New York," *Public Interest* (Fall 1986), p. 4.

21. *Arizona Daily Star*, March 20, 1987, p. 12. Meanwhile, governmental housing support changed from assisting an annual average of 300,000 new households during 1976–80 to adding less than half that many households during 1981–86. As a result, by 1986 nearly 800,000 fewer households received housing assistance than would have otherwise, had the policies prior to 1981 continued in place.

22. *Time Magazine*, February 2, 1987, p. 26.

23. This paragraph is based on Robert Greenstein, "The Decreasing Effectiveness of Anti-poverty Programs, 1979–1985," Center on Budget and Policy Priorities, November 25, 1986, pp. 1–2, Tables 1 and 2.

24. Numerous studies dealing with the impact of public assistance on work effort and unemployment are reviewed and discussed in Sheldon Danziger et al., "How Income Transfer Programs Affect Work, Savings, and Income Distribution: A Critical Review," *Journal of Economic Literature* (September 1981).

25. Even the experimental guaranteed income programs had only a marginal impact upon most males, reducing the number of hours worked by about 9 percent. See Charles Murray, *Losing Ground: American Social Policy, 1950–1980* (New York: Basic Books, 1984), pp. 150–152. See also Chapter 2, above, note 67, for other studies on guaranteed income programs.

26. In 1980 a total of 401,000 black males aged 16–24 were unemployed, representing one in eleven of nearly 4.3 million unemployed males over age 15. In 1983 the figures were 524,-000 and 6.3 million, respectively. Bureau of Labor Statistics, *Handbook of Labor Statistics*, June 1985, pp. 65–66, Table 26.

27. See notes 24 and 25, above.

28. Glen Cain, "Comments on Murray's Analysis of the Impact of the War on Poverty on the Labor Market Behavior

of the Poor," Institute for Research on Poverty, Special Report No. 38, University of Wisconsin, Madison, August 1985, mimeo, p. 21.

29. Calculated from Bureau of the Census, *SAUS:* 1982–83, p. 380, Table 632. Of an increase of 1.1 million employed workers aged 16–19 from 1965 to 1970, 840,000 got part-time jobs. In 1965 only about 40 percent of the employed workers aged 16–19 held part-time jobs.

30. For some examples of the growth of jobs by occupational classification in the 1970s, see Chapter 3, note 39.

31. For the growth of the employed work force, see President of the United States, *Economic Report of the President, 1986,* p. 288, Table B-31, for figures through 1985. For 1986, see Council of Economic Advisors, *Economic Indicators,* January 1987, p. 11.

32. The figures are from Barry Bluestone and Bennett Harrison, "The Grim Truth About the Job Miracle," *New York Times,* February 1, 1987, section 3, p. 1. For a more detailed presentation of the wages of jobs created between 1979 and 1984, see Barry Bluestone and Bennett Harrison, "The Great American Job Machine: The Proliferation of Low Wage Employment in the U.S. Economy," prepared for the Joint Economic Committee of the U.S. Congress, December 1986.

A contrary view—that the number of decent paying jobs increased no less in the Reagan years 1981–85 than in the 1977–81 years or the 1973–77 years—is found in Warren T. Brookes, "Low-Pay Jobs: The Big Lie," *Wall Street Journal,* March 25, 1987, p. 32. Yet even Brookes' analysis shows that the total number of jobs created from 1981 to 1985 declined by one-quarter compared with 1977–81, dropping from 9.2 million in the Carter years to 6.8 million in the Reagan years. This 25 percent decline corresponds closely to the rise by 33 percent from 1981 to 1985 in the number of Americans working part-time because they could not find satisfactory full-time employment.

33. Council of Economic Advisors, *Economic Indicators,* January 1987, p. 11.

34. Ibid., p. 13.

35. The comparisons in this and the following three paragraphs are calculated from the following sources: for 1980–86, Council of Economic Advisors, *Economic Indicators,* January 1987, p. 2 (GNP), p. 17 (industrial production), p. 6 (per capita disposable income), p. 11 (employment), p. 9 (gross private investment and nonresidential investment), p. 10 (investment in plant and equipment), p. 16 (nonfarm business productivity), and U.S. Department of Labor, *Monthly Labor Review,* September 1986, p. 86, Table 44 (manufacturing productivity); for 1970–80, President of the United States, *Economic Report of the President, 1986,* p. 254, Table B-2 (GNP), p. 304, Table B-45 (industrial production), p. 283, Table B-26 (per capita income), p. 288, Table B-31 (employment), p. 252, Table B-1 (gross private investment and nonresidential investment), p. 311, Table B-51 (investment in plant and equipment), p. 302, Table B-43 (nonfarm business productivity), and U.S. Department of Labor, *Monthly Labor Review,* September 1986, p. 86, Table 44 (manufacturing productivity). The 1970s here includes 1980.

Whenever two periods are compared, the risk of arbitrary selectivity of the periods enters into the picture. I attempt to address this issue by making two sets of comparisons between the present and the past—the 1980s compared with the 1970s (each compared to the other in its entirety) and the years of economic recovery in the 1980s compared with the years of the last economic recovery of the 1970s. Despite this, a problem still remains. There is no known way accurately to ascertain the influence that the earlier period has had on the later one. Although impossible to measure accurately, economic developments in the 1970s undoubtedly did influence developments to some degree in the early years of the 1980s, and to ever lesser degrees thereafter.

36. Sources for the comparisons between 1983–86 and 1976–78 in this and the following paragraphs are cited in note 35.

37. Robert S. McIntyre and Dean C. Tipps, "Exploding the Investment Incentive Myth," *Challenge,* May/June 1985, p. 50.

38. Cannon, *Reagan,* p. 332.

39. McIntyre and Tipps, "Investment Incentive Myth," p. 50.

40. The remainder of the paragraph is calculated from ibid., pp. 48–50.

41. Ibid., p. 50.

42. The president's own Council of Economic Advisors takes a similar view. It finds that from the beginning of the recovery, in 1983, the recovery was demand-led, far more so than in any other industrial country. See President of the United States, *Economic Report of the President, 1987,* pp. 101–2; see also Wallace Peterson and Paul S. Estenson, "The Recovery: Supply Side or Keynesian," *Journal of Post Keynesian Economics* (Summer 1985).

43. For 1983–86, see Council of Economic Advisors, *Economic Indicators,* January 1987, p. 10. The author has adjusted for inflation.

44. Cannon, *Reagan,* p. 328.

45. Changes in energy prices, 1973–86, may be found in President of the United States, *Economic Report of the President, 1986,* p. 320, Table B-59, and Council of Economic Advisors, *Economic Indicators,* January 1987, p. 24, for 1986.

46. Isabel V. Sawhill and Charles F. Stone, "The Economy: The Key to Success," in Palmer and Sawhill, *The Reagan Record,* p. 80, Table 3.1.

47. Allen Sinai, "The Soaring Dollar Did It," *Challenge,* October 1985, pp. 20–21.

48. Calculated from Gregory B. Mills, "The Budget: The Failure of Discipline," in Palmer and Sawhill, *The Reagan Record,* p. 110, Table 4.2.

49. Estimates indicate that the deficits following 1981 would have been no lower, and probably would have become larger still, had President Reagan's various budget proposals been enacted entirely without change. See Mills, "The Budget," pp. 108–17, and David A. Stockman, *The Triumph of Politics: The Inside Story of the Reagan Revolution* (New York: Avon, 1987), pp. 429–35.

50. Calculated from President of the United States, *Economic Report of the President, 1986*, p. 339, Table B-73.

51. Figures on the size of the federal debt compared with the GNP in this and the next paragraph are calculated from ibid.

52. See Chapter 3, pp. 75–85.

53. The findings of the president's commission are described in Chapter 2, p. 63–64.

54. Even the Grace Commission report on cost control in government, when subjected to scrutiny, did not yield sums close to the advertised savings. An analysis of the Grace Commission report by the Congressional Budget Office found that reduced expenditures in domestic programs would be modest. After subtracting reductions in the deficit that would be generated from defense savings, from new *revenues* the report calls for (from increased taxes, user fees, and the sale of federal property), from savings in the retirement program for federal employees, and from savings in interest that would be attached to these actions, the remaining savings that the report pinpoints in all domestic programs for the public—savings that would result in a reduction of expenditures—amounted to an estimated $53.4 billion over three years, or $17.8 billion for a single year. The total amounts to about 3 percent of spending. This percentage is similar to the one found by the House Republicans in 1979 (see above, Chapter 2, p. 62–63). Even then, part of these savings would be as much a matter of lowering services (a policy decision) as of bringing about the delivery of the same services at improved cost and efficiency. For example, the Grace Com-

mission called upon the government to limit growth in health care costs to the growth of the GNP. In attempting to carry out such a policy, controlling government spending on health care in the face of higher than average inflation in the health sector would likely lead to the provision of fewer health services. For the Congressional Budget Office analysis, see U.S. Congress, Congressional Budget Office and General Accounting Office, *Analysis of the Grace Commission's Major Proposals for Cost Control,* February 1984.

55. Figures on net interest as a percentage of federal revenues are calculated from President of the United States, *Economic Report of the President, 1986,* p. 345, Table B-78. The percentage started rising rapidly in 1980 owing primarily to the rise in interest rates stemming from the oil-fueled inflation of 1979–80. Net interest as a percentage of federal revenues was 9.4 percent in 1980 and 8.4 percent in 1979. In 1965 the figure was 6.8 percent.

56. Gerald Epstein, "What Hath Conservative Economics Wrought?" *Challenge,* July/August 1986, p. 46.

57. For comparisons of real interest rates after 1980 with those of 1949–69, 1969–73, 1973–79, see Epstein, "Conservative Economics," p. 41.

58. President of the United States, *Economic Report of the President, 1986,* p. 373, Table B-105; and Sinai, "The Soaring Dollar Did It," p. 19.

59. In 1987 the president's own Council of Economic Advisors came to this same conclusion. See President of the United States, *Economic Report of the President, 1987,* p. 111.

60. C. Fred Bergsten, "Presentation," U.S. Congress, Joint Economic Committee, *A Symposium,* January 16–17, 1986, p. 691.

61. William Schneider, "The New Shape of American Politics," *Atlantic Monthly,* January 1987, p. 43.

62. Murray L. Weidenbaum, "Economic Prospects for 1986," speech delivered to the Annual Correspondents Conference, St. Louis, Missouri, November 14, 1985, in *Vital*

*Speeches of the Day,* City News Publishing, February 1, 1986, p. 243.

63. Stockman, *The Triumph of Politics,* p. 447.

### Epilogue: Looking Back to the Future

1. Alexis de Tocqueville, *Democracy in America,* J. P. Mayer and Max Lerner, eds. (New York: Harper & Row, 1966). See also John Dewey, *The Public and Its Problems* (Denver: Swallow, 1927).

2. Lester M. Salamon and Alan J. Abramson, "The Nonprofit Sector," in John L. Palmer and Isabel V. Sawhill, eds., *The Reagan Experiment: An Examination of Economic and Social Policies Under the Reagan Administration* (Washington, D.C.: Urban Institute Press, 1982), p. 222, Table 7–1.

3. Ibid.

4. Lester M. Salamon, "Nonprofit Organizations: The Lost Opportunity," in John L. Palmer and Isabel V. Sawhill, eds., *The Reagan Record: An Assessment of America's Changing Domestic Priorities* (Cambridge, Mass.: Ballinger, 1984), p. 267, Table 8–1.

5. Joseph A. Pechman, *The Rich, the Poor, and the Taxes They Pay* (Brighton, Eng.: Wheatsheaf Books, 1986), p. 22, Table 1.2.

6. The point might be made that the elderly could have avoided poverty in their old age by earning and saving when they were younger. Yet this point ignores the fact that during their prime earning years in the 1950s, those now over age 65 were working in a private economy which left more than one-quarter of all Americans in poverty (in 1955), and many more at little above that. Even with governmental assistance included, still nearly one in four Americans lived in poverty in 1955. See Charles Murray, *Losing Ground: American Social Policy, 1950–1980* (New York: Basic Books, 1984), p. 65, Figure 4.5. In addition, retirement plans as part of one's employment were much less common in the 1950s, and a number

of the employee retirement plans that did exist were badly managed. Going broke, these plans left those depending on them for retirement stranded, some paying out not even a single penny.

7. A discussion of the philosophical argument and literature on this point is found in Robert E. Goodin, *Protecting the Vulnerable* (Chicago: University of Chicago Press, 1985), pp. 109–53.

8. Even were there enough jobs so that those who are now unemployed became employed, upward economic mobility in America would not soon lift most of them into decent-paying jobs. In America today, only one in five sons of laborers whose own first job is a laborer *ever* rises to any white-collar job whatsoever or to a blue-collar job that is any higher than an operative. For 80 percent of Americans at the lower end of the ladder, economic mobility has slowed nearly to a halt. Calculations based on Alan C. Kerchhoff, Richard T. Campbell, and Idee Winfield-Larid, "Social Mobility in Great Britain and the United States," *American Journal of Sociology* 95, no. 2 (1985), pp. 302–7, Tables A-1, A-2, A-3.

9. See Chapter 2, pp. 31–36, and Chapter 6, pp. 157–161.

10. Two examples of recent public opinion polls (by Yankelovich and Roper) that demonstrate this popular view are reported in *Time*, March 30, 1987, p. 37 and *The Washington Post National Weekly Edition*, June 8, 1987, p. 38.

11. For some other ideas for welfare reform that are well worth consideration, see Daniel P. Moynihan, *Family and Nation* (New York: Harcourt Brace Jovanovich, 1986); Alice M. Rivlin, ed., *Economic Choices, 1984* (Washington, D.C.: Brookings Institution, 1984), especially pp. 157–71; and Ben W. Heineman, Jr., et al., *Work and Welfare: The Case for New Directions in National Policy* (Washington, D.C.: Center for National Policy, 1987). For a review of proposals for welfare reform, see Arnold Gurin, "Welfare Reform: Review of Proposals," Florence Heller Graduate School for Advanced·

Studies in Social Welfare, Brandeis University, February 1987, mimeo.

12. In the proposed public assistance program, the top incomes would remain as they are—still many times above those at the median—and the bottom incomes, even when raised to the poverty line, will still be only about one-third of the median income. Retaining the philosophy undergirding the free market system, these income differentials leave plenty of room for individual incentive.

13. About half the states give no aid to two-parent families, regardless of how poor the families are, and few states give direct income assistance to families whose head is employed, once more no matter how much the family's income falls beneath the poverty line. Moreover, in many states, the benefits that are granted to recipients are themselves well beneath the poverty level, even when food stamps and the available housing assistance are included. Medicaid also presently excludes up to half of the poor in some states. It would be available to all (above and beyond poverty-level income grants) under the proposed reform.

14. People who do not enroll in a workfare program or are unwilling to comply with its rules would not receive public assistance. This is not to say that such people could receive no aid. Private organizations would be completely free to help persons who are unwilling to comply with the conditions for public assistance. At the same time, a reformed public assistance program would need to provide assurance that both applicants and current recipients gain effective protection and remedies against the possibility of arbitrary decisions by officials regarding who should and should not receive public assistance. Workfare would also need to be based on reasonable expectations. To illustrate, while many mothers in nonpoor families are employed, two-thirds have jobs requiring less than 30 hours a week. It would not be reasonable to require greater employment of single mothers

than mothers in two-parent families find it prudent to do.

15. This paragraph is based on House of Representatives, Committee on Ways and Means, *President's AFDC Work Proposals and the White House Domestic Policy Council Evaluation of Federal Welfare Programs,* 99th Cong., 2nd sess., February 27, 1986, p. 123, Table 3.

16. Ibid., pp. 127–28, Tables 4 and 5, and Laura A. Kiernan, "Massachusetts' Jobs Program Doesn't Work for Everybody," *Washington Post National Weekly Edition,* March 2, 1987, p. 15.

17. These programs and literature describing their results are reported above in Chapter 2, pp. 44–47, and notes 55–62 of Chapter 2.

18. For a description of the New Hampshire results and how they contrast with other well-known workfare programs, see Warren T. Brookes, "The Stunning Failure of Dukakis's ET," *Wall Street Journal,* January 19, 1987. Whereas the welfare caseload declined by 30 percent from 1983 to 1986 in New Hampshire, the caseload under the Education and Training Program (ET) in Massachusetts did not decline at all in the same period.

19. The figures on the level of AFDC assistance to recipients of the San Diego program are based on data reported in Committee on Ways and Means, *President's AFDC Work Proposals,* p. 123, Table 3, to which standard food stamp assistance was then added.

20. In addition, the costs do not include governmental expenditures for industrial development—to stimulate emerging industries and help revive old ones—so as to generate more and better-paying jobs in the private economy.

21. Quoted in Helen Dewar, "Democrats Are Charging Full Speed Ahead More Slowly," *Washington Post National Weekly Edition,* March 23, 1987, p. 11.

22. For example, at $395.9 billion, personal and corporate income taxes amounted to 9.9 percent of GNP in 1985, whereas in 1955 personal and corporate income taxes totaled

$46.6 billion, or 11.7 percent of GNP, and in 1960 they totaled $62.2 billion, or 12.4 percent of GNP. The difference between 1985 and the earlier years amounts to around 2 percent of GNP, or $80 billion if GNP is at $4 trillion, as it was in 1985. A similar figure results if personal income is used as the base rather than GNP. See President of the United States, *Economic Report of the President, 1987*, p. 244, Table B-1 (for GNP in 1985), and p. 333, Table B-74 (for personal and corporate taxation in 1985); Bureau of the Census, *SAUS: 1965*, p. 324, Table 444 (for GNP in 1955 and 1960), and p. 396, Table 534 (for personal and corporate taxes in 1955 and 1960). In 1980, personal and corporate income taxes as a proportion of the GNP amounted to 11.7 percent, exactly the same as in 1955.

23. Another issue of concern in the proposal is that in order to help poor Americans the reformed program calls for assisting nonpoor Americans. It assists nonpoor Americans in ever decreasing amounts as the income level of a household comes closer to the median income. Understandably, Americans are reluctant to have government assist people who are above the poverty line. Yet one important reason to do so is to avoid the injustice that some people would otherwise end up with as much from the community as other people, working full-time, would derive from their own efforts. Another reason is that while the poor are the most in need, they are not the only people in need. Other Americans in our free market system also face harsh economic circumstances that are beyond their own control. One of the least recognized of these groups, for example, is the crowded baby boom generation itself, the generation whose influence on economic and social developments in America has been so crucial to the growth of the misperceptions upon which our policies rest today. To look at their situation is to see why assistance granted even to people who are above the poverty line but below the median income would not be money misspent.

Contrary to the image of the younger generation as a privileged group of Americans who own expensive condos, cars, and clothes, the baby boomer generation has been forced to live within extremely stringent, below-average budgets. Their financial hardships are a direct outgrowth of the gigantic size of the generation. Their large numbers simultaneously put downward pressures on wage levels in exchange for the creation of new jobs and upward pressures (as a result of increased demand) on the costs of major fixtures such as housing. This at a time when two oil crises sent energy prices skyrocketing, causing inflation that further reduced real incomes.

The result was dramatic. Consider the remarkably different situations facing two males, one who reached age 30 in 1959 and another who reached age 30 in 1973. (This and the following two paragraphs are based on Richard C. Michel, "An Economic Bust for the Baby Boom," *Challenge,* March/April 1986, pp. 34–38.) A male of age 30 in 1959 would by age 40, in 1969, have received a real increase in earnings averaging 49 percent (from $17,188 to $25,627 in constant 1984 dollars); in sharp contrast, the earnings of a similar male of age 30 in 1973 would have declined a little by age 40 in 1983 ($23,580 in 1973 and $23,395 in 1983 in constant 1984 dollars). A male of age 40 in 1983 was actually earning about 15 percent less in real terms than was the equivalent male of the same age ten years earlier.

Yet even while earning 15 percent less in 1983, expenses had risen sharply. Most important, the cost of housing had risen from 21 percent of monthly earnings in 1973 to 41 percent of monthly earnings in 1983. Energy costs (utilities, gas, and motor oil) rose by another 6 percent of earnings.

To deal with these pressures, younger families had to make numerous sacrifices. These families have bought or rented far smaller housing than did equivalent families a decade earlier; they also cut back elsewhere by spending 30 percent *less* on clothes, 14 percent less on furniture, and 15 percent less on personal care; they had fewer children; an increasing number of spouses got jobs; they gave 38 percent less to charity; and they cut savings fourfold to just 1 percent of income. Fewer than one-fifth of the crowded baby boom generation are the proverbial yuppie. Rather than being a privileged class, the majority of members of the baby boom generation are people who work hard and receive less. It is a group of Americans whose lower earners, even when above the poverty line, can sorely use help to ease a burden that is not of their own making, and one which has grown heavier with time. Under the proposed reform of public assistance, such people whose incomes are below the median would get help rather than remain ignored as they are today. Also, others who live on equally stringent budgets would receive help. Rather than expanding access to assistance, we are presently curtailing governmental programs that help non-poor Americans with below-average incomes.

### Appendix Pollution Control: The Need for Governmental Involvement

1. Milton Friedman and Rose Friedman, *Free to Choose* (New York: Avon Books, 1981), p. 204.

2. Ibid.

3. Council of Environmental Quality, *Environmental Quality, 1979* (Washington, D.C.: U.S. Government Printing Office, 1979), pp. 674–78.

4. William Drayton, Jr., "Comments on Regulatory Strategies for Pollution Control," in Ann F. Friedlander, ed., *Approaches to Controlling Air Pollution* (Cambridge, Mass.: MIT Press, 1978), pp. 233–34.

5. Ibid., pp. 234–35. C. S. Russell also warns of the sizable problems that may be involved in administering a pollution-tax system in "What Can We Get From Affluent Charges?" *Policy Analysis,* vol. 5, no. 2, pp. 155–80.

6. James A. Fay, "Comments to Government Policies Toward Automotive Emissions Control," in Friedlander, *Approaches to Controlling Air Pollution*, p. 411.

7. A. Myrick Freeman III, "Technology-Based Effluent Standards: The U.S. Case," *Water Resources Research* 16, no. 1 (February 1980), p. 27.

# Index

# Index

# Index

# Index

# Index

# Index

# Index

# Index

# Index

# Index

# Index

# Index

# Index

# Index

DATE DUE